P9-DUD-949

TABLE OF CONTENTS

DEDICATION

To Beverly

My dear wife, counselor, and confidant, who sacrificially gave ten years of her life in order that I might prepare for an effective ministry among my people. Her dedication to Christ has been an inspiration and encouragement for the past twenty-five years of my Christian pilgrimage.

PREFACE

You have just picked up one of the most fascinating studies ever penned by a prophet. Joel presents a comprehensive overview of God's prophetic program for Israel in just three chapters.

But why write on Joel, when other Old Testament books present a more comprehensive treatment of Israel in prophecy?

Why Joel? Because it is a neglected book. Although Joel is included in all the Old Testament commentary sets, few individual commentaries are available for study. Those in print are often too scholarly for most people, who get lost in the technical language, or are too shallow for a serious student desiring a more comprehensive treatment of the text.

Why Joel? Because it is one of the most abused books in the Bible. Some commentators neglect to interpret Joel in its proper historical, grammatical and cultural setting, thus arriving at fallacious interpretations of the text. Such phrases as "the day of the Lord" (1:15), "I will pour out my Spirit upon all flesh" (2:28), "former rain and the latter rain" (2:23), and "I will restore to you the years that the locust hath eaten" (2:25) have been misinterpreted or misapplied. Other commentators, while interpreting Joel in its proper setting, wrongly teach that the prophecy is to be fulfilled in the Church.

Why Joel? Because many Christians are either wrongly taught or confused concerning Israel's place in God's prophetic program. Some hold that the promises made in the Abrahamic Covenant were forfeited when Israel sinned against God; thus the promises are being fulfilled in the Church. This is not so! The Abrahamic Covenant was based upon God's sovereign purposes and power for fulfillment, and not the faithfulness of Abraham or his seed. The future fulfillment of the provisions given to Israel in the Abrahamic Covenant are confirmed in Joel's prophecy.

Why Joel? Because the book presents a chronology of Israel's prophetic history from the Babylonian captivity to the Millennial Kingdom. Without a proper grasp of the role Israel plays in God's program, one will be susceptible to theological error and false teaching on prophecy today.

Why Joel? Because a pattern emerges in this book concerning God's dealings with the Gentiles. Nations are on a collision course which will culminate at Armageddon. In descriptive terms, Joel presented the destiny of the nations as they relate to Israel in the Day of the Lord.

Here is profit for today from the prophet of yesterday. Author David Levy, himself a Hebrew Christian, has presented keen insight into this important portion of God's Word. Not only is the commentary clear and concise, but each chapter begins with a full-page chart to give added insight into the prophetic message of the Book of Joel.

In order to comprehend the message of this book, it is imperative that the student pray for divine guidance. Take a moment before turning the page and ask God for understanding of what you are about to read. Pray that God will impart the spiritual message He has for you from the pages of this timely prophetic book.

Marv Rosenthal
Executive Director
THE FRIENDS OF ISRAEL
GOSPEL MINISTRY, INC.

INTRODUCTION

The book of Joel bears its author's name and means *Jehovah is God.* Little is known concerning Joel's background with the exception that his father was Pethuel (1:1). Although his residence was not given, most likely he came from Judah and resided in Jerusalem. Some scholars have suggested that Joel was a priest, but this is highly doubtful for he does not include himself with them (1:13-14; 2:17). Luke confirms Joel to be one of the prophets of Judah (Acts 2:16).

Joel did not date the time of his writing. It is commonly held by conservative Bible scholars that he wrote sometime between 838-756 B.C. There are two reasons for holding these dates. First, he made no mention of either the Assyrian (722 B.C.) or Babylonian (587 B.C.) invasions of Israel. Second, the period is preferred since no king was mentioned in the book. This would coincide with the time Queen Athaliah had the royal seed of Judah murdered. After the death of King Ahaziah, Queen Athaliah had all her grandchildren put to death, but the baby Joash was spared (the only surviving royal seed). He was hidden by his aunt Jehosheba and Jehoiada, the high priest, in the Temple complex. Seven years later Joash was crowned king of Judah (2 Ki. 11:12), and Queen Athaliah was slain by her own people (2 Ki. 11:16). The book could have been written just prior to Joash's coronation in 835 B.C.

Joel wrote to the nation of Judah and particularly to the city of Jerusalem (3:1, 17), prophesying against the Temple, its priesthood, and its offerings (1:9). When Joel mentioned the name Israel, he did not refer to the ten tribes in the northern kingdom, but to the twelve tribes during *the day of the Lord* (3:2, 14).

The theme of Joel is *the day of the Lord* (1:15; 2:1, 11, 31; 3:14). Although the theme is introduced by Obadiah (v. 15), Joel is the one who develops it. The phrase, *the day of the Lord,* has reference to the direct intervention of God in the affairs of man. The theme has a twofold meaning. First, the phrase, *day of the Lord*, refers to God's judgment which came upon Judah after Joel penned the prophecy. Second, it has reference to the Tribulation period which will culminate in Christ's coming in glory and the establishment of His Millennial Kingdom.

Not only will *the day of the Lord* be a time of judgment on Israel's enemies but a time of great blessing to the righteous in Israel who will enjoy the Millennial Kingdom.

OUTLINE

I. INSECT PLAGUE (1:1-20)

A. Declaration of the Lord (vv. 1-3)
B. Destruction by the Locust (vv. 4, 6-7)
C. Discouraging Lament (vv. 5, 8-14)
D. Day of the Lord (v. 15)
E. Drought on the Land (vv. 16-20)

II. INVASION PREDICTED (2:1-11)

A. The Alarm Sounded (vv. 1-2)
B. The Army's Strength (vv. 4-9)
C. The Awesomeness Seen (vv. 3, 10)
D. The Armies of the Savior (v. 11)

III. INTERCESSORY PRAYER (2:12-17)

A. Plea for Repentance (v. 12)
B. People are to Repent (vv. 13-16)
C. Priests are to Repent (v. 17)

IV. INTERVENTION PROMISED (2:18-27)

A. Pity on the Lamenters (v. 18)
B. Promise to the Lamenters (v. 20)
C. Protected by the Lord (v. 19)
D. Prosperity from the Lord (vv. 19, 21-27)

V. RETURN OF MESSIAH (2:28-32)

A. Spirit's Indwelling (vv. 28-29)
B. Signs of Invasion (vv. 30-31)
C. Salvation for Israel (v. 32)

JOEL 1:1-20

The word of the Lord that came to Joel, the son of Pethuel. Hear this, ye old men, and give ear, all ye inhabitants of the land. Hath this been in your days, or even in the days of your fathers? Tell ye your children of it, and let your children tell their children, and their children another generation. That which the palmer worm hath left hath the locust eaten; and that which the locust hath left hath the cankerworm eaten; and that which the cankerworm hath left hath the caterpillar eaten. Awake, ye drunkards, and weep; and wail, all ye drinkers of wine, because of the new wine; for it is cut off from your mouth. For a nation is come up upon my land, strong, and without number, whose teeth are the teeth of a lion, and he hath the cheek teeth of a great lion. He hath laid my vine waste, and barked my fig tree; he hath made it completely bare, and cast it away; its branches are made white.

Lament like a virgin girded with sackcloth for the husband of her youth. The meal offering and the drink offering are cut off from the house of the Lord; the priests, the Lord's ministers, mourn. The field is wasted, the land mourneth; for the grain is wasted; the new wine is dried up, the oil languisheth. Be ye ashamed, O ye farmers; wail, O ye vinedressers, for the wheat and for the barley, because the harvest of the field is perished. The vine is dried up, and the fig tree languisheth; the pomegranate tree, the palm tree also, and the apple tree, even all the trees of the field, are withered, because joy is withered away from the sons of men. Gird yourselves, and lament, ye priests; wail, ye ministers of the altar; come, lie all night in sackcloth, ye ministers of my God; for the meal offering and the drink offering are withheld from the house of your God.

Sanctify a fast, call a solemn assembly, gather the elders and all the inhabitants of the land into the house of the Lord, your God, and cry unto the Lord. Alas for the day! For the day of the Lord is at hand, and as a destruction from the Almighty shall it come. Is not the food cut off before our eyes, yea, joy and gladness from the house of our God? The seed is rotten under their clods, the garners are laid desolate, the barns are broken down; for the grain is withered. How do the beasts groan! The herds of cattle are perplexed, because they have no pasture; yea, the flocks of sheep are made desolate. O Lord, to thee will I cry; for the fire hath devoured the pastures of the wilderness, and the flame hath burned all the trees of the field. The beasts of the field cry also unto thee; for the rivers of waters are dried up, and the fire hath devoured the pastures of the wilderness.

A VISUALIZED OUTLINE - PART ONE

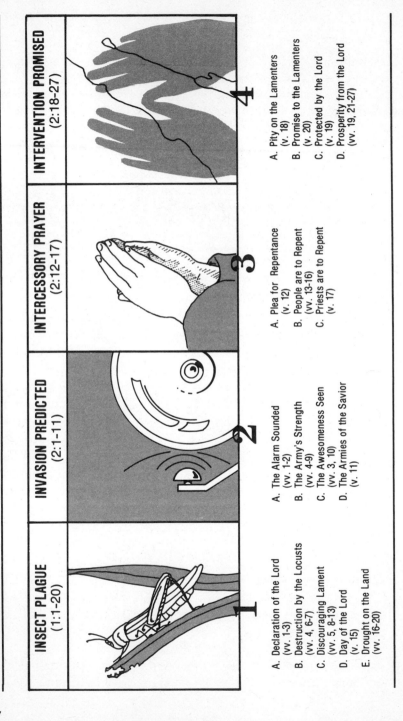

INSECT PLAGUE (1:1-20)	INVASION PREDICTED (2:1-11)	INTERCESSORY PRAYER (2:12-17)	INTERVENTION PROMISED (2:18-27)

A. Declaration of the Lord (vv. 1-3)
B. Destruction by the Locusts (vv. 4, 6-7)
C. Discouraging Lament (vv. 5, 8-13)
D. Day of the Lord (v. 15)
E. Drought on the Land (vv. 16-20)

A. The Alarm Sounded (vv. 1-2)
B. The Army's Strength (vv. 4-9)
C. The Awesomeness Seen (vv. 3, 10)
D. The Armies of the Savior (v. 11)

A. Plea for Repentance (v. 12)
B. People are to Repent (vv. 13-16)
C. Priests are to Repent (v. 17)

A. Pity on the Lamenters (v. 18)
B. Promise to the Lamenters (v. 20)
C. Protected by the Lord (v. 19)
D. Prosperity from the Lord (vv. 19, 21-27)

1

THE DAY OF THE LORD: INSECT PLAGUE

Joel 1:1-20

The twentieth century man can sit comfortably in his home and, via television documentaries, watch the devastation which war leaves in its wake. He sees masses of humanity slaughtered and made refugees, buildings leveled, land denuded of its life, and a ghostly gray haze hovering over the ravaged area — an awesome sight indeed! Many of these men are retired soldiers who spend hours swapping stories of war-torn countries in which they have served.

Joel was not swapping war stories with the elders of Judah. Nor was he speaking about a nation destroyed by the ravages of war, but in a sense something worse! He was prophetically sounding out a message from God (v. 1) concerning an awesome plague which was about to totally devastate Judah.

DECLARATION OF THE LORD (vv. 1-3)

Insect plagues were nothing new to the Middle East, and it was no less so in Judah. Joel prefaced his prophecy with a question to the inhabitants of Judah. "Hear this . . . Hath this been in your days, or even in the days of your fathers?" (v. 2). *Have you known such a swarm of locusts?*

The elders and inhabitants of Judah were well-versed in the past. Stories of plagues, calamities and wars were

rehearsed over and over from generation to generation —
with every detail memorized. Very vivid in the Israeli mind
were the plagues which centuries before descended on the
Egyptians. Yet, nothing of this dimension, duration or
destruction had been known to the elders.

Thus, Joel said, "Hear" (v. 2), to both elder and inhabitant.
*Open your ears, hear every word, compare the stories of your
forefathers; for I will tell you of a devastation more awesome
than you can imagine.*

Moses had instructed Israel to rehearse the works of God
to their children (Dt. 4:9; 6:6-7) for two reasons: first, so they
might remember the goodness and mercy of God toward
them in times of their disobedience; second, to remind them
that God would judge sin if they became disobedient (Lev.
26; Dt. 28). "Tell ye your children of it . . . and their children
another generation" (v. 3), said Joel, in order that they might
learn to be obedient to the Lord.

DESTRUCTION BY THE LOCUSTS (vv. 4, 6-7)

The locusts are pictured as a huge army swarming upon the
land (v. 6). Their teeth are compared to those of a lion. Like
the lion, locusts have a strong bite and great power, grinding
their food, completely destroying whatever they eat. The
palmerworm gnaws off or shears away; the *locust* swarms in
mass, destroying everything in its path; the *cankerworm* licks
off; and the *caterpillar* devours or consumes by stripping
away (v. 4). They have stripped both grapevine and fig tree
clean, even eating the bark until the branch stood white in its
nakedness (v. 7). Though Joel only mentioned four species of
locust, over eighty species are known to exist in the East.

Those in the Middle East call locusts "the army of god."
As an army, they march in a regular order, camp in the field at
night, and in the morning rise with the sun, dry their wings,
and fly in the direction of the wind (Prov. 30:27; Nah. 3:16-
17). They number in the billions (Jer. 46:23), covering an
area up to ten miles in length and five miles wide, and have
been known to fly seventeen hours at a time, covering over

fifteen hundred miles. Their vast number can blot out the sun bringing a temporary darkness over the earth (Joel 2:2, 10; Ex. 10:15). Nothing stops them — not ditch, fire, wall, door, or window (Joel 2:7-9). Their appetite is never satisfied; they devour all the vegetation in their path. [1]

The locusts are symbolic of those invading nations who will come upon Judah destroying the land as presented in verses six and seven.

DISCOURAGING LAMENT (vv. 5, 8-14)

The message of the plague was directed to five groups in Judah. First, God called the drunkard to awaken from his stupefying intoxication to see the destruction coming upon the land. "Awake, . . . weep; and wail, all ye drinkers of wine," (v. 5) said Joel. They were called to lament the cutting off of their source of wine. The quick and best cure for alcoholism is to remove the source of the drink — this God did!

Alcoholism is a downfall to any nation. In the United States it is the number one drug problem and the number three health problem. There are 18 million alcoholics and problem drinkers in the country today. Each year drinkers are involved in one million traffic accidents resulting in 28,000 deaths and 500,000 injuries. Over fifty-five percent of all highway deaths are alcohol related. Alcohol is a contributing factor in thirty-one percent of all homicides, thirty-six percent of all suicides, thirty-one percent of nonauto accidents, and seventy-five percent of all crimes. Alcohol costs the American economy over 25.3 billion dollars annually. In 1974, only one in eight families was being affected by alcohol; today it is one in four. [2]

The drunkard, awakening from his stupor, is a picture of Israel awakening from her stupefaction of sin. Sin, like alcohol, dulls the senses, binds the individual under its control, insensates to what is right and wrong, and completely dominates the life of the individual. Like the drunkard, Israel was to awaken, weep and wail over her spiritual loss.

Second, He spoke to the nation as a whole. Israel was to

"Lament like a virgin girded with sackcloth for the husband of her youth" (v. 8). She is pictured as a virgin who has just consummated her marriage and, on that very day, loses her husband through death. This is the most tragic and bitter mourning one could experience.

With every joy put away, Israel, like a virgin bereaved of her husband, was to drape herself in sackcloth. She was to wear the formless, coarse, black goats' hair garment next to her skin, wailing out over her condition as the coarse garment chafes at her body. In this manner, Israel would show contrition of heart and sorrow of soul for her sin against God.

Third was the mourning of priests and ministers (v. 9). Why? Because the loss of "grain . . . new wine . . . [and] oil" (v. 10) made the grain and drink offerings impossible (v. 9). Thus, their livelihood was cut off since they depended upon the ministry of the Temple for their provision.

Fourth, the farmer stood ashamed after losing everything (v. 11). "Ashamed" means that they turned pale when seeing how the locusts had stripped their fields clean, for they depended upon the wheat and barley for their livelihood. With destruction of their crops, desolation of the land, God's disfavor, and no access to the Temple services, the farmer must have felt destitute.

Fifth, the vinedressers "wailed" (v. 11) over their loss when the grapevine dried up and the fig tree languished. But other trees suffered as well. The pomegranate, palm (not subject to injury), and apple trees were destroyed as well. Even the mighty trees of the forest succumbed to the locusts and withered.

With the withering of the tree came the withering of Israel's joy (v. 12). Whenever the vintage and harvest were poor or destroyed, the people of Judah were unable to rejoice (Isa. 16:10). But this was more than a poor harvest! Joel expresses the complete devastation with such words as "cut off" (v. 9), "wasted" and "languisheth" (v. 10), "perished" (v. 11), "dried up" and "withered" (v. 12).

The spiritual leaders were required to bring the offering of true repentance. First, they were to put on sackcloth as a symbol of the inward sorrow felt because of their sin (v. 13). Second, they were to lie in sackcloth all night, wailing in prayer, because of their sin and the loss of Temple offerings (v. 13).

The priests, as representatives of elders and people, were to gather them together in a *solemn assembly* for the purpose of *fasting* and *crying unto the Lord* over their sin (v. 14). The proclamation of a fast and solemn assembly was commonplace in Israel and the surrounding nations during a time of distress or impending disaster. Nineveh is a good example of a brutal people, an idolatrous city, who called a fast, put on sackcloth, repented of their sin, and turned back to God (Jon. 3:5). God spared them for one hundred years from total destruction.

A number of years ago the Ninety-Third Congress of the United States called for a national day of fasting, humiliation and prayer. The people were to humble themselves before their Creator, acknowledge dependence upon Him, and repent of their individual and national sins. Little real turning to God resulted from this proclamation, as evidenced by the conditions existing today in this country. But repentance must be forthcoming if God is to withhold His hand of judgment. The city of Nineveh is a clear example of a people who heeded the warning from God and were spared. But the nation which closes its ears to the prophetic pronouncement will eventually suffer God's judgment.

DAY OF THE LORD (v. 15)

Joel described this awesome day as *the day of the Lord* (Jehovah). The phrase *day of the Lord* is used some five times in Joel (1:15; 2:1; 2:11; 2:31; 3:14). Although it has reference to the local judgment God would bring on Judah through this plague, it speaks of a future day when God will intervene in judgment upon the world. For example, Joel 2:31 must be speaking of a future day of judgment, because the sun was not darkened, nor the moon turned into blood during Joel's

day. Again, Joel 3:14 does not speak of Joel's day but a future
day of judgment upon the enemies of Israel. The plague in
Joel's day was a prototype of an awesome *day of the Lord* yet
future.

To understand what is meant by *the day of the Lord,* one
must understand the difference between *man's day* and the
Lord's day. There are four key days mentioned in Scripture.
First is *man's day.* This phrase is used in 1 Corinthians 4:3 in
reference to "man's judgment." Paul said: "But with me it is
a very small thing that I should be judged of you, or of *man's
judgment* . . . ." This "man's judgment" is literally *man's day,*
having reference to the day which now is, when men have
control over human government.

Second is *the day of Christ,* mentioned six times in Scripture (1 Cor. 1:8; 5:5; 2 Cor. 1:14; Phil. 1:6, 10; 2:16). It refers
to the time when Christ will come to rapture the Church (1
Th. 4:13-18) out of the earth, taking Christians to be with
Him (Jn. 14:1-3) forever.

Third is *the day of the Lord,* which speaks of a dark gloomy
day (2:1) — a time of judgment. *The day of the Lord* refers to
the direct intervention of God in the affairs of man after the
Rapture of the Church. It covers the Tribulation (Rev. 6-19),
Millennial Kingdom (Rev. 20:1-10), and the Great White
Throne Judgment (Rev. 20:11-15). It is not only a time of
judgment on the wicked, but a time of great blessing for the
redeemed of Israel and the Church.

Fourth is *the day of God,* mentioned in 2 Peter 3:12, which
has reference to the heavens passing away, the elements
melting, the earth being renovated by fire, and the establishment of a new heaven and earth, ushering in the eternal state.

The words, "destruction from the Almighty" (Heb. *Shod*
and *Shaddai*) [v. 15], come from the Hebrew word *Shadad.*
It is a play on words showing the comparison between the
individual (God) who will cause the destruction and the
literal destruction (Keil and Delitzsch, *Minor Prophets,* Vol. I,
p. 187).

DROUGHT ON THE LAND (vv. 16-20)

The judgment upon Judah affected every aspect of the land. First, their food supply was destroyed right before their eyes as the locusts reaped it for themselves (v. 16). Second, the prospect for future food was nonexistent because of the total destruction from the locusts and the drought which would ensue (v. 17). The seed was rotten under its clod because the drought and hot sun destroyed the shoots the moment they appeared. Thus, the garners, with nothing to harvest, allowed the barns to lay in disrepair. Third, the blazing sun burned up the pastures, scorched the trees and dried up the rivers (vv. 18-19).

Without pasture and water, the beasts would not survive for long. The animal world suffered because of man's sin and cried out for deliverance (v. 18). Paul tells us "that the whole creation groaneth and travaileth in pain together until now" (Rom. 8:22), waiting for the day when it will be delivered (Rom. 8:19, 21; Isa. 65:25). Adam's sin affected all of creation, because it was under his domain, but at Christ's Second Coming creation will be delivered.

There was a greater calamity to be suffered by Judah than that which the locusts would do! A nation might well be able to stand a destructive force which rips their land in pieces, if they have the joy and comfort of the Lord. But a people who have been cut off from their God have little hope.

Judah had little hope! The "joy and gladness" which they had known at the house of the Lord had been removed (v. 16). This was only a foretaste of the future despair Judah would face when God would bring complete judgment on her (Isa. 1-5; Lam. 2), for Judah was to lose everything, land, city and Temple; but, worst of all, they would lose the blessings and comfort they had known in their covenant relationship with God.

Lessons are to be learned from Judah's experience. Christians living in the United States enjoy unprecedented peace, prosperity and plenty as no other nation on the earth.

One should not take these blessings lightly. But this nation is on a destructive course! In fact, someone has stated that if God does not judge America, He will have to apologize to Sodom and Gomorrah. In a moment of time God could remove His hand of blessing, judgment could fall and loss ensue as it did in Judah.

Annie Walker, an eighteen-year-old girl, saw the urgency of the hour in 1854. After reading the Lord's words in John 9:4, "I must work the works of him that sent me, while it is day; the night cometh, when no man can work," she quickly penned the well-known hymn, "Work for the Night is Coming." The night of this world is soon approaching. Christian friend, be like Ezekiel whom God set as a *watchman* in his day: hear the *Word* of God, and *warn* the people to turn back to God (Ezek. 33)!

JOEL 2:1-11

Blow the trumpet in Zion, and sound an alarm in my holy mountain. Let all the inhabitants of the land tremble; for the day of the Lord cometh, for it is near at hand; A day of darkness and of gloominess, a day of clouds and of thick darkness, like the morning spread upon the mountains; a great people and a strong; there hath not been ever the like, neither shall be any more after it, even to the years of many generations. A fire devoureth before them, and behind them a flame burneth; the land is like the garden of Eden before them, and behind them a desolate wilderness; yea, and nothing shall escape them. The appearance of them is like the appearance of horses; and like horsemen, so shall they run. Like the noise of chariots on the tops of mountains shall they leap, like the noise of a flame of fire that devoureth the stubble, like a strong people set in battle array. Before their face the peoples shall be much pained; all faces shall gather blackness. They shall run like mighty men; they shall climb the wall like men of war, and they shall march every one on his ways, and they shall not break their ranks. Neither shall one thrust another; they shall walk every one in his path, and when they fall upon the sword, they shall not be wounded. They shall run to and fro in the city; they shall run upon the wall; they shall climb up upon the houses; they shall enter in at the windows like a thief. The earth shall quake before them; the heavens shall tremble; the sun and the moon shall be dark, and the stars shall withdraw their shining: And the Lord shall utter his voice before his army; for his camp is very great; for he is strong who executeth his word; for the day of the Lord is great and very terrible, and who can abide it?

DAYS MENTIONED IN THE BIBLE

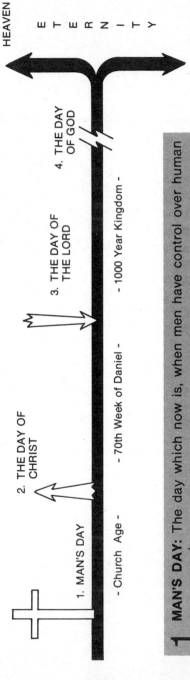

1. **MAN'S DAY:** The day which now is, when men have control over human government.

2. **THE DAY OF CHRIST:** The day when Christ comes to Rapture the Church out of the earth.

3. **THE DAY OF THE LORD:** The day when God takes direct control in the affairs of men extending from the Rapture of the Church to the Great White Throne Judgment.

4. **THE DAY OF GOD:** The day when the heavens pass away and the earth is renovated by fire, and a new heaven and earth usher in the eternal state.

2

THE DAY OF THE LORD: INVASION PREDICTED

Joel 2:1-11

Like the keen-eyed Ezekiel, Joel was a watchman over the nation of Judah. The word of warning burned within him as a Jeremiah ready to come forth in prophetic proclamation concerning God's wrath. Feeling the winds of judgment on the horizon, in pungent prophetic tones Joel steps up his impassioned plea: "Blow the trumpet in Zion" (v. 1).

THE ALARM SOUNDED (vv. 1-2)

Upon the walls of Jerusalem stood the alert sentry, always watchful, with trumpet (shofar) in hand, ready to sound the alarm of impending danger. But here the warning was to be sounded from a different platform. The message will be heralded from "Zion," the "holy mountain" (v. 1), which has reference to Mount Moriah, where Solomon's Temple stood. The priest (v. 15), not the soldier, was to blow the shofar — and not as a military alert, but to gather Judah for individual and national repentance (vv. 12-17) — for the Temple was the abode of God's presence, the place to beseech Him in prayer and fasting, in the hope that He would divert the judgment.

The effect of blowing a shofar from Zion would strike fear in the people causing the whole land to "tremble" (v. 1). *Is a horn blown in a city without the people being scared?* (Amos 3:6) asked Amos. Like an air raid siren, with the blowing of the shofar comes the warning, "for the day of the Lord cometh, for it is near at hand" (v. 1). The word "cometh" literally means *has come.* Although the judgment is still future, in God's eyes it has already taken place.

Why did *the day of the Lord* strike terror in the Judean? Because it will be a day filled with "darkness and of gloominess, a day of clouds and of thick darkness" (v. 2). These words express the character of this day on which God will judge. The darkness is compared to that of the "morning spread upon the mountains" (v. 2). Some believe this was speaking of the somber yellow light from the yellow wings of the locusts being reflected off the mountains. But the metaphor was saying, *As dawn suddenly covers a large area on the mountaintop, so shall this plague of locusts suddenly darken the whole earth.* In chapter one, Joel described the locust swarm as being so dense that it blotted out the light of day. Such was the case during the locust plague in Egypt (Ex. 10:15).

Joel, speaking hyperbolically, expressed the awesomeness and complete devastation which would take place when God pours out judgment on Judah: ". . . there hath not been ever the like, neither shall be any more after it, even to the years of many generations" (v. 2).

Naturally, this was not the most severe destruction to come upon the land. During the Great Tribulation, God will pour out a holocaust on the whole world. Daniel spoke of that day: ". . . and there shall be a time of trouble, such as never was since there was a nation even to that same time..." (Dan. 12:1).

Jesus predicted that the Great Tribulation would be the worst holocaust ever known to man. "For then shall be great tribulation, such as was not since the beginning of the world to this time, no, nor ever shall be" (Mt. 24:21).

Think of a period in human history, and this time of judgment shall be worse! One might say, *What about the time of Noah's flood when all flesh outside of the ark perished?* True, all flesh outside of the ark died, but the vegetation survived, the earth was not completely destroyed. The Great Tribulation will be greater in its effect on all of creation, especially in the duration of pain and suffering which man will undergo. In fact, Jesus said, "And except those days should be shortened, there should no flesh be saved; but for the elect's sake those days shall be shortened [cut off]" (Mt. 24:22). He was saying, *If the Tribulation were any longer than seven years, nothing would live — man, animal or vegetation.*

THE ARMY'S STRENGTH (vv. 4-9)

The locust plague descended on Judah like a massive, well-equipped cavalry, moving toward a single objective, that of destruction. First, the locusts looked like horses (v. 4). In fact, the Italian word for locust is *cavalette (little horse),* and the Germans use the word *heapforde (hay horse)* in referring to them. This was not new, for Theodoret said centuries ago, "If any one should examine accurately the head of a locust, he will find it exceedingly like that of a horse." [1]

Second, they not only resembled horses, but horsemen (v. 4) in their swiftness, as they rushed to devour with devastating judgment. There is an old Arab saying that declares, "In the locust, slight as it is, there is the nature of ten of the larger animals — the face of a horse, the eyes of an elephant, the neck of a bull, the horns of a deer, the chest of a lion, the belly of a scorpion, the wings of an eagle, the thighs of a camel, the feet of an ostrich, the tail of a serpent." Some might call this an oriental exaggeration, but ask those who have suffered from the devastating power of the locust, and you will see the truth of this picture. [2]

Third, the sound of their movement is expressed in two ways. The sound of their springing and leaping was like that of a two-wheeled war chariot rumbling over the rocky Judean mountains. Their feeding pierced the air like the crackling of a burning bush or dried stubble (v. 5). [3]

Fourth, they came dressed in "battle array" (v. 5) leaving

the impression of a military horde outfitted for battle with helmet and flexible mail covering.

Fifth, Joel quickened the pulse of his expression as he described the onslaught of this army of locusts. He said, "They shall run like mighty men" (v. 7); that is, they came like a corps of commandos, in high morale, charging their enemy with vigor and valor. They came like "men of war" (v. 7). No wall was too impregnable, no obstacle could deter their advance, only victory was anticipated as they pressed on to the prize before them. They came relentlessly in irresistible order, "they shall walk every one in his path" (v. 8), and "they shall not break their ranks" (v. 7). They were not deterred from their objective, neither did they straggle along, but moved with impelling instinct as one massive body which had the appearance of being directed by an organized leader, but they had none (Prov. 30:27).

With parade-ground precision, in steady advance, they came. The city of Jerusalem was theirs in which to "run to and fro" (v. 9) at will. Nothing escaped them! They scaled walls, clung to houses, ground, clothes, food and people; all was covered by them.

Sixth, there was no force that could stay their progression, for "when they fall upon the sword [lit. *among the darts*], they shall not be wounded" (v. 8). Man has used every known means to stop them, but to no avail. One writer expressed it this way, "Their number was astounding; the whole face of the mountain was black with them. On they came like a living deluge. We dug trenches, and kindled fires, and beat and burned to death heaps upon heaps, but the effort was utterly useless. Wave after wave rolled up the mountainside, and poured over rocks, walls, ditches, and hedges, those behind covering up and bridging over the masses already killed. After a long and fatiguing contest, I descended the mountain to examine the depth of the column, but I could not see to the end of it." [4]

To those who faced and fought the locust plague in Judah, it seemed like a living hell on earth. But this was a vivid type of a more vicious locust plague which will descend on the whole earth during the Great Tribulation. In that day, the fifth trumpet of judgment will be blown (Rev. 9:1) and with it will be opened the bottomless pit, out of which will emerge smoke so dense that it will darken the atmosphere, blotting out the light of day (Rev. 9:2). Coming out of this black pit of Hell will be a swarm of locusts (Rev. 9:3) which almost defies description. Their look will be horrifying! They will come forth "like horses prepared unto battle; and on their heads were, as it were, crowns like gold, and their faces were like the faces of men. And they had hair like the hair of women, and their teeth were like the teeth of lions. And they had breastplates, as it were breastplates of iron; and the sound of their wings was like the sound of chariots of many horses running to battle. And they had tails like scorpions . . ." (Rev. 9:7-10).

Are these real locusts? No, since they will not feed on grass or any green thing, but will sting men like scorpions for five months — those who are without the seal of God in their foreheads (Rev. 9:4).

Then who are they? They are demonic spirits which will take on this strange body, so vile and wretched that they will have been chained in the bottomless pit for centuries (Jude 6), so vile and wicked that they could not be allowed freedom to roam the earth. Their king will be none other than Satan himself, who is called *Abaddon* in Hebrew and *Apollyon* in Greek (Rev. 9:11), meaning the *destroyer*.

The locusts will use their tails to sting all unsaved people on earth for five months (Rev. 9:3, 5, 10). The sting will be so painful in its agony and duration that people will try to commit suicide in order to be relieved of their torment. For people to seek death shows the severity of their torment, but death will flee from them (Rev. 9:6). Here is a picture of the final Hell that awaits them in eternity! Men will be tormented without relief, desiring to die, only to find their suffering to be eternal.

Notice, this horrible locust plague, as well as the sixth

trumpet judgment (Rev. 9:13-20), will not bring repentance! In fact, mankind will become more vile, manifesting his wickedness without restraint. He will be given over to a reprobate mind which will express itself in the worship of demons, idolatry, murders, sorceries, fornication and theft (Rev. 9:20-21). Earth will be a living hell!

THE AWESOMENESS CITED (vv. 3, 10)

The land of Judah was lush and green like the garden of Eden (v. 3) before the plague. But after the locusts passed through the land, it was "desolate wilderness" (v. 3). Not one blade of green foliage could be seen. In fact, it looked like a land devoured by fire (v. 3).

What happened to Judah will be worldwide during the Tribulation. The lush green portions of the earth will become a desolate wilderness. In the first part of the Tribulation, war will have its impact upon the land preventing the production of enough food to feed the masses of humanity. The result can only be death by famine (Rev. 6:3-8). As the Tribulation progresses, more of the earth will be destroyed. The first trumpet judgment will be devastating, leaving one third of the earth's vegetation in total destruction (Rev. 8:7).

The horde of locusts affected the heavens as well as the earth. Joel said, ". . . the heavens shall tremble; the sun and moon shall be dark, and the stars shall withdraw their shining" (v. 10). Naturally, the locusts, even though vast in number, cannot affect the heavens and earth as described above, but the terror of this devastating judgment will strike such fear in the people that it will seem as if the earth is quaking under their power; the heavens will tremble with the sound of their flying; and the sun, moon and stars will be darkened by their vast number which will blot out the light.

Even though Joel is using figurative hyperboles to express the horrible terror of this locust plague, there is a prophetic parallel that will take place in the Tribulation. During the Tribulation there will be three great earthquakes (Rev. 6:12; 11:13; 16:18-19) which will affect the heavens (Mt. 24:29;

Rev. 12-14).

With the swarm of locusts descending upon Judah, Joel records the reaction of the people as "pained; all faces shall gather blackness" (v. 6). The people were struck with terror at the sight of the locusts, inner pain gripped them, they turned pale and trembled, knowing the awesome destruction which awaited them. But not so in the Tribulation! With the final judgment being poured out on man, the testimony of John was that "men blasphemed God because of the plague" (Rev. 16:21).

THE ARMIES OF THE SAVIOR (v. 11)

The locust plague, although literal, is illustrative of a futuristic judgment which is to come on Israel. God had spoken, but His people turned a deaf ear to the warning; now He will speak to their enemies.

Joel gave a threefold description of the terror God's instruments manifest toward His people. First, "his camp is very great" (v. 11); the armies God will use to chasten His people will be massive. Second, "for he is strong who executeth his word" (v. 11); the massive armies will move as one force, like a locust plague, to do the bidding of God's command. Third, "for the day of the Lord is great and very terrible, and who can abide it?" (v. 11). Implicit in the question is the answer — no one, unless the Lord shows mercy!

Who is this "army" (v. 11) of the Lord? It will be both the Assyrians and Babylonians described as the "northern army" (v. 20). First were the Assyrians, who uprooted the ten tribes of the northern kingdom of Israel in 722 B.C. carrying them off into captivity (2 Ki. 17:1-41). They brought in Gentiles to replace the Israelites, who married the poorer people left in the land. This resulted in a corrupt religious system which was a mixture of Judaism and paganism. The group became known as Samaritans, who later persecuted the Jews coming back from the Babylonian captivity.

Second was the collapse of the southern kingdom of Judah

during the Babylonian captivity of 586 B.C. Nebuchadnezzar reduced Jerusalem and Solomon's Temple to rubble (2 Ki. 25:1-30). Judah was taken back to Babylon for the seventy year captivity prophesied by Jeremiah (Jer. 25:11).

A still greater fulfillment of this horrible *day of the Lord* is yet to be seen during the Great Tribulation. At that time the nations of the world will again converge on Israel (Zech. 14:2) with a horrible campaign of battles ensuing called "the battle of that great day of God Almighty" (Rev. 16:14). But the verdict of this war will not be the total destruction of Israel, for the Lord will go forth and fight against those nations who have come up to do battle (Zech. 14:3), destroying them with the word of His mouth (Rev. 19:15).

Seeing the destruction left by the Babylonians, Jeremiah cried, "It is because of the Lord's mercies [loving-kindness] that we are not consumed . . ." (Lam. 3:22). Who can "abide the day of the Lord?" asked Joel. Only those who have experienced the LOVING-KINDNESS of the Lord.

HAVE YOU?

JOEL 2:12-17

Therefore also, now, saith the Lord, turn even to me with all your heart, and with fasting, and with weeping, and with mourning; And tear your heart, and not your garments, and turn unto the Lord, your God; for he is gracious and merciful, slow to anger, and of great kindness, and repenteth him of the evil. Who knoweth if he will return and repent, and leave a blessing behind him, even a meal offering and a drink offering unto the Lord, your God?

Blow the trumpet in Zion, sanctify a fast, call a solemn assembly. Gather the people, sanctify the congregation, assemble the elders, gather the children, and those that nurse at the breasts; let the bridegroom go forth from his chamber, and the bride out of her room. Let the priests, the ministers of the Lord, weep between the porch and the altar, and let them say, Spare thy people, O Lord, and give not thine heritage to reproach, that the nations should rule over them. Why should they say among the people, Where is their God?

TIMES OF THE GENTILES

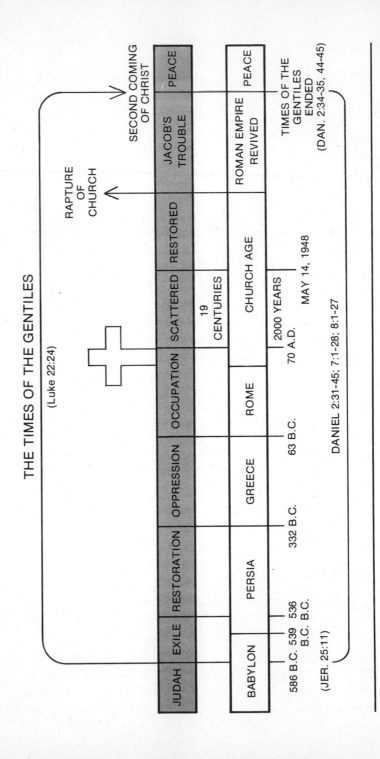

THE TIMES OF THE GENTILES

(Luke 22:24)

3

THE DAY OF THE LORD: INTERCESSORY PRAYER

Joel 2:12-17

Judah was on the verge of expiring! Her spiritual chart read: head sick, heart faint, body full of wounds, bruises and putrefying sores. From head to toe there was no soundness in her, cried Isaiah (Isa. 1:6).

Not even by offering the proper sacrifice would God remove Judah's sin and provide spiritual healing, for He said: *I cannot bear your sacrifice; I am weary of your appointed feasts; I will hide my eyes and close my ears to your prayers* (Isa. 1:11-15)! All was a postured pretense in worship, a shameful sham, and a sick stench in the nostrils of God.

Could there be any hope for Judah? Yes, if Judah would come and reason her spiritual condition before the Lord, there was hope. God set forth the choice: *Repent and obey Me, and ye shall eat the good of the land; refuse and rebel, and ye shall be devoured by the sword.* The choice hinges on, "If ye be willing" (Isa. 1:18-20).

PLEA FOR REPENTANCE (vv. 12-14)

Joel put the same choice before Judah years earlier. The plea was urgent, "Therefore . . . now . . . turn even to me . . ." (v. 12). "Therefore" reflects back to everything prophesied up to that point concerning the locust plague which was about to descend upon Judah. Joel was saying, *You see the imminent danger, "now . . . turn," in hope that God will stay His hand of judgment. Turn in repentance with a contrite heart, not with an external show of sacrificial worship.*

Repentance comes from a Hebrew word which means *to draw a deep breath,* as one does in expressing relief or sorrow. With reference to man's sin, repentance is that inner contrition and conviction which leads the individual to confess and forsake his sin. True repentance involves contrition of heart, confession with the mouth and a change in the person's conduct.

CONTRITION

The repenter must show sincere contrition over his sin which will affect him in three ways. First, contrition affects the *intellect.* To repent means *to have a change of mind* about one's sin. A changed mind is clearly illustrated during Peter's sermon on the day of Pentecost, when he said, ". . . Repent, and be baptized, every one of you, in the name of Jesus Christ for the remission of sins . . ." (Acts 2:38). The Jewish people had viewed Jesus as a false Messiah, but now their eyes were opened; 3,000 *repented* (had a changed mind) of their sin and became believers. Upon hearing Peter's message, their intellect was changed by the Holy Spirit (Acts 2:14-36).

Second, contrition affects the *will.* It is not enough to be intellectually convicted or convinced of sin, there must be the will to confess and forsake it. This is beautifully portrayed by the willful action of the prodigal son (Lk. 15:11-32). Seeing the degraded state into which he had gotten himself, the prodigal son made the *willful choice* to abandon the pigpen of sin, return to his father and confess his sin (Lk. 15:17-21).

Third, contrition affects the *emotions.* David caught the true spirit of contrition when he said, "The sacrifices of God are a broken spirit; a broken and a contrite heart, O God, thou wilt not despise" (Ps. 51:17).

Those in Judah were to manifest this type of contrition. God said, "turn . . . with fasting . . . weeping . . . mourning;

And tear your heart, and not your garments" (vv. 12-13). By *fasting,* the Judean humbled himself before God, which heightened his sensitivity and sorrow over sin, producing a deeper reliance on the Lord. By *weeping and mourning* (lit., *beating one's breast)* [v. 12], he showed to God and others his grief felt over sin. Jesus' parable of the praying Pharisee and publican presents a beautiful contrast of true weeping over sin. When the Pharisee prayed, he extolled his virtues before God; but the poor publican, never looking up from his position in a corner of the Temple, beat his breast as he confessed his sin with great contrition of heart (Lk. 18:13). By *tearing his garment,* the Judean presented an outward sign of the inner grief he felt over sin. But it was possible to rend the garment without having true contrition for one's sin. God is saying, *Do not just give Me the outward motion of grief, but show your emotional brokenness over sin with a rent heart.*

Contrition is more than feeling sorrow or remorse over sin. When Judas saw that he was condemned after betraying Jesus, he "repented" (Mt. 27:3). In this context, the word "repent" (K.J.V.) is better translated *remorse.* Judas did not really repent (change his mind about the sin), but only sorrowed over his action. His mental anguish drove him to commit suicide. On the other hand, Peter went out and "wept bitterly" after his denial of Jesus (Mt. 26:75), which was an expression of true contrition and repentance over his sin.

Jesus said, "Blessed are they that mourn; for they shall be comforted" (Mt. 5:4). The truly contrite, who mourns over his sin, will be a blessed (happy) man and receive comfort from the Lord.

CONFESSION

True contrition leads the individual to *confession* of his sin. Confession is to admit one's guilt and agree with God that, in fact, he has transgressed God's Law. The Levitical Law required, along with confession, that restitution be made to the offended party, whenever possible, before remission was granted (Lev. 5:5-6; Num. 5:7; Lev. 16:21).

Unconfessed sin has a destructive effect on the individual, spiritually, psychologically and physically. David attested to this fact in the year he carried his unconfessed sin with Bathsheba. Spiritually, he lost the joy of his salvation, feeling the presence of the Lord had left him (Ps. 51:11-12). Pyschologically, his sin was continually before him (Ps. 51:3). Physically, David felt his strength ebbing away during the time he hid his sin (Ps. 32:3-4; 51:8). Not until he acknowledged his sin through outward confession was the burden lifted; then he sensed forgiveness and the joy of his salvation returned (Ps. 32:1; 51:3; 2 Sam. 12:13).

Before God can forgive the Christian, he must confess and forsake his sin (1 Jn. 1:9), and make reconciliation with an offended brother whenever possible (Mt. 6:14-15; 18:15-17).

CONDUCT

True confession leads to a *changed conduct.* This was beautifully illustrated at the Thessalonians' conversion — when they "turned to God from idols, to serve the living and true God" (1 Th. 1:9). Their change in conduct was manifested in three ways. First, they "turned to God," meaning a conversion took place. They were headed in one direction, made an about-face, and went in the opposite direction. Second, they "turned . . . from idols." Literally, they turned *away from* the sinful practices of their past idolatry, never to worship that way again. Third, they "turned . . . to serve the living and true God." They became slaves, or bondservants to Christ. Notice, they did not just make adjustments in their conduct, but a radical change took place which was expressed in total commitment to the Lord. True repentance produces this type of change — the change God desired of Judah, if their repentance was to be valid.

God expects the same commitment of the believer today! There *must be* true confession of sin from a contrite heart, followed by a change in conduct, if the believer's repentance is to be acceptable before God. "For the grace of God . . . hath appeared to all men, Teaching us that, denying ungodliness and worldly lusts, we should live soberly, righteously, and godly, in this present age" (Ti. 2:11-12), said Paul.

But what assurance did the Judeans have that God would hear the sinner's prayer? Like a father to a wayward son, God desired to bring reconciliation between Himself and Judah. Joel aimed to awaken Judah to this fact by reminding them that God is "gracious and merciful, slow to anger, and of great kindness" (v. 13). The words "gracious and merciful, slow to anger, and of great kindness" are used in other portions of Scripture as a creedal statement for God's grace unto Israel (Num. 14:18; Ps. 86:15; Jon. 4:2; Nah. 1:3).

God's *graciousness* is the foundation of His *mercy,* and because of His mercy, He is *slow to anger* (longsuffering), which manifests itself in *great kindness* (abundant goodness) toward His people. Israel's history is punctuated with God's mercy toward them: David (2 Sam. 24:14), Solomon (1 Ki. 3:6; 8:23), Nehemiah (Neh. 9:19), and Jeremiah, after the Babylonian destruction (Lam. 3:22), all experienced the loving-kindness of the Lord.

If only Judah would repent of her evil, God would repent of the evil (judgment) of her (v. 13). But how can a perfect God repent? Does God change His mind?

In answering these questions, a distinction must be made between God's *nature, character* and *action* toward man. The nature and character of God are immutable, meaning there is no variableness or change within Him. God's attributes work together in perfect harmony, they cannot contradict each other, "he abideth faithful; he cannot deny himself" (2 Tim. 2:13). It cannot be said that God changes His purpose or mind when it comes to bringing judgment on sin. But God will change His action (withhold judgment) when a person or nation truly repents. Therefore, repentance on God's part involves a proper divine reaction to man's sin — that is, God will either extend mercy or judgment.

If Judah repented, would God stay His hand of judgment? Joel, not wanting to give a definite answer, says, "Who knoweth" (v. 14), meaning *perhaps* God will remove the judgment. Although God promises to take away eternal damnation from all who repent of their sin, He still reserves the right to bring or remove temporal judgment on an individual or nation. This is illustrated in two instances of repentance. First, when David sinned with Bathsheba, God forgave his sin (2 Sam. 12:13), but the temporal consequences of David's sin would follow him the rest of his life (2 Sam. 12:10). Second, Nineveh had sinned greatly, but God took away their sin and restrained His hand of temporal judgment (Jon. 3:9-10). The same principle holds true for the Christian: His sin is taken away, but many times he reaps the results of his sin (Gal. 6:7-8).

Would there be an indication from God that Israel's repentance had been accepted? Yes, He would again restore the grain and vineyard, which had been cut off (1:9, 13, 16), in order for Judah to offer a meal and drink offering (v. 14).

How can the Christian know that his repentance is acceptable to God? Simply by believing the authority of God's Word, "If we confess our sins, he is faithful and just to forgive us our sins, and to cleanse us from all unrighteousness" (1 Jn. 1:9). A right relationship with God will be manifested through a cleansed life which produces fruit and radiates the joy of the Lord (Jn. 15:1-11).

THE PLACE OF REPENTANCE (vv. 15-17)

Joel had already called the people to the Temple for repentance (1:14; 2:1), but in greater detail he spells out what is involved in their coming to petition God. The nation was instructed to fast, not only individually (v. 12), but in a "solemn assembly" (v. 15). The fast indicates a corporate self-humiliation as a nation before God in hope that the coming judgment might be averted.

All the *people* were required to come without exception: "... elders ... children ... those that nurse ... bridegroom ... and the bride" (v. 16). The crisis was so serious that those who would normally be exempt from worship, because of age or a recent marriage, were required to gather to fast and pray.

It must be remembered that all are sinners, no matter what their age or standing in society.

The *priests* were to plead in prayer "between the porch and the altar" (v. 17). They were to stand facing the door of the holy place entreating the Lord with weeping and pleading, hoping He would show mercy and avert the judgment.

Joel instructs the priests how to intercede on behalf of the nation. They were to pray, "Spare thy people, O Lord" (v. 17). Judah was God's people and possession by His direct sovereign choice (Dt. 7:6). This was not the first time in which a plea of intercession for Israel had been made; Moses (Ex. 32:12; Dt. 9:28-29) and Joshua (Josh. 7:6-9) offered the same plea.

They were to pray, "and give not thine heritage to reproach, that the nations should rule over them" (v. 17). A better translation of this prayer would be, "And do not make Thine inheritance a reproach, A *byword* among the nations" (N.A.S.B.).

There are two reasons why the verse was not speaking of Judah's fear that nations would rule over them. First, the context of Israel's fear concerns the locust plague which was ready to descend in destruction, not heathen nations. Second, if Judah were destroyed by the locusts, they would become a "reproach, A byword among the nations," thus bringing reproach to God and His glory. Why would this be so? Because the nations would surmise that Israel's God was either unconcerned so would not deliver her, or, worse, lacked the power to do so. Therefore, the heathen would say, "Where is their God?" (v. 17), scoffing, mocking and trampling the true and living God underfoot.

Today, like then, God is "longsuffering toward us, not willing that any should perish, but that all should come to repentance" (2 Pet. 3:9). God shows loving forbearance in manifesting judgment, hoping that it will lead men to repentance.

One day God's longsuffering will run out, and *the day of the Lord* will come in devastating judgment. A holocaust like this world has never experienced is fast approaching. Is there any hope for sinful men? Yes, a genuine repentance and turning to Christ. Is there any hope for America? Yes, the same hope which God put before Judah and every other nation that went off in sin. The choice is clearly one of repentance or ruin. The country is on a collision course and has a date with destruction unless repentance is forthcoming. In Judah, repentance began at the house of the Lord. God will not accept anything less from His people today.

JOEL 2:18-27

Then the Lord was jealous for his land, and pitied his people. And the Lord answered and said unto his people, Behold, I will send you grain, and wine, and oil, and ye shall be satisfied with them; and I will no more make you a reproach among the nations, But I will remove far off from you the northern army, and will drive him into a land barren and desolate, with his face toward the eastern sea, and his rear toward the western sea, and his stench shall come up, and his ill savor shall come up, because he hath done great things.

Fear not, O land. Be glad and rejoice; for the Lord will do great things. Be not afraid, ye beasts of the field; for the pastures of the wilderness do spring, for the tree beareth her fruit, the fig tree and the vine do yield their strength. Be glad then, ye children of Zion, and rejoice in the Lord, your God; for he hath given you the former rain moderately, and he will cause to come down for you the rain, the former rain and the latter rain in the first month. And the floors shall be full of wheat, and the vats shall overflow with wine and oil. And I will restore to you the years that the locust hath eaten, the cankerworm, and the caterpillar, and the palmer worm, my great army which I sent among you. And ye shall eat in plenty, and be satisfied, and praise the name of the Lord, your God, who hath dealt wondrously with you; and my people shall never be ashamed. And ye shall know that I am in the midst of Israel, and that I am the Lord, your God, and none else; and my people shall never be ashamed.

RUSSIA WITH ALLIES ATTACK ISRAEL

EASTERN EUROPE
(Gomer)

RUSSIA
(Gog and Magog)
(Togarmah*)

IRAN
(Persia)

ETHIOPIA
(Cush)

ISRAEL

LIBYA
(Put)

Ezekiel 38-39
(Probably During First Half
of Tribulation)

*Probably Turkey and Armenia

4

THE DAY OF THE LORD: INTERVENTION PROMISED

Joel 2:18-27

Will God answer the repentant plea of a nation marked out for judgment? The cynic says, *No!* The religionist says, *I hope so!* The believer responds in faith, *God will!*

Will God? What saith the prophet? Jeremiah said to Judah, "If that nation, against whom I have pronounced, turn from their evil, I [God] will repent of the evil that I thought to do unto them" (18:8). Amos hopefully proclaimed to Israel, "Seek ye me [God], and ye shall live" (5:4). Jonah reluctantly declared to Nineveh, ". . . God repented of the evil that he had said that he would do unto them, and he did it not" (3:10). To Solomon God promised, "If my people, who are called by my name . . . turn from their wicked ways, then will I hear from heaven . . . and will heal their land" (2 Chr. 7:14). Yes, God will forgive the sins and stay His hand of judgment toward a people who turn in repentance. Such was the case with Judah in the days of Joel.

PITY ON THE LAMENTERS (v. 18)

The Lord heard the pleading petition of His people and had pity on them. He is more sensitive to the cry of Israel than a mother for her child. In fact God says a mother might forget to show compassion on her nursing child, but the Lord will not forget Israel. So concerned is God for Israel that He even engraved their name upon the palms of His hands (Isa. 49:15-16).

God is touched deeply by the affliction of His people. Isaiah stated, "In all their affliction he was afflicted, and the angel of his presence saved them; in his love and in his pity he redeemed them; and he bore them, and carried them all the days of old" (Isa. 63:9). Who is this "angel of his presence"? It is none other than Jesus the Messiah! Yes, Jesus, the Rock that followed them in the wilderness (1 Cor. 10:4-5), the One who has sustained them in their trials and persecutions throughout the centuries.

God loves Israel so much that He is "jealous for his land" (v. 18). His eye is continually on it in protective care throughout the year (Dt. 11:12). One can imagine how it grieved the heart of God to bring judgment on Israel. For nineteen centuries the land lay in disarray, deserted by its people, until the sons of Jacob returned to restore it in this century.

Lest Israel take credit for the removal of judgment, Joel reminds her that it was the Lord who "pitied his people" and delivered them from destruction.

PROMISE TO THE LAMENTERS (v. 20)

God promised to remove the enemy referred to as the "northern [lit., *northerner*] army" (v. 20). Is the *northerner* to be interpreted as locust or man?

Locust plagues have been known to descend upon Jerusalem from the north (e.g., 1915 plague), but this is rare. Usually they come riding on the winds which blow from the south or southeast. A northern plague of locusts could have been driven into the barren and desolate Negev, where God would destroy them, causing a great stench to prevail over the land (v. 20). Jerome reports seeing locusts, which had been drowned in the Mediterranean Sea, piled in a stinking heap from three to four feet high, stretching for fifty miles along the shoreline. But nowhere in the Bible are locusts referred to as the *northerner,* nor does Scripture ever make reference to them performing "great things" (v. 20). [1]

The word *north* is used as a technical term in the Old Testament apocalyptic sections to typify the enemies of Israel: Assyria, Babylon, and others coming on her in the latter days (Isa. 14:31; Jer. 1:14-15; 4:6; 6:1, 22; Ezek. 38:6, 15; 39:2; Zeph. 2:13). Thus, the imagery in verse twenty changes from that of locust to a mighty army poised to come down on Israel. [2]

Although God did deliver Judah from the locust plague and the Assyrians (Isa. 36-39) in answer to prayer, this section looks toward a greater time of deliverance in the latter days.

Who is this army mentioned in verse twenty? Ezekiel describes a huge confederacy of nations who will descend upon Israel from the north in the latter days (Ezek. 38:3; 39:2). The confederacy will be made up of Magog (Russia), Persia (Iran), Libya, Ethiopia (in North Africa), Gomer (Germany), and Togarmah of the north quarters (Turkey and Armenia) [Ezek. 38:2, 5-6].

When will the army descend? It must be in the "latter days" (Ezek. 38:8, 14, 16, 18; 39:8, 11) when Israel will be dwelling safely (Ezek. 38:8) without bars or gates (Ezek. 38:11). The only time Scripture mentions a time when Israel is dwelling safely (before the Lord's return) is during the first half of the Tribulation. At that time, the Antichrist will make a covenant of peace with Israel (Dan. 9:27) guaranteeing her protection from surrounding enemies. But after three and a half years of peace the Antichrist will break this covenant, turn on Israel, and start to persecute all who will not worship him and his image which will be erected in the Tribulation Temple. Most likely, this huge army will descend from the north sometime near the middle of the Tribulation.

Why will this army come against Israel? For three basic reasons. The first reason is because of *location.* Israel is in the midst of the nations (Ezek. 5:5; Dt. 32:8), a land bridge between Europe, Asia and Africa. The one who controls

Israel would be strategically positioned to have a controlling impact on the above continents. This location would give Russia a central military base, control over Middle East oil flowing to the west, domination of Israel's government (changing it from a democracy to a socialistic state), supremacy to govern Israel's worship of God, and many ideal places for warm water ports on the Mediterranean coastline. Second, Russia would control the *mineral wealth of the Dead Sea* which is an inestimable fortune. Third, a huge deposit of *oil* may be discovered in Israel which the Russians would want to control. Only oil would bring great and instant wealth to Israel (Ezek. 38:13).

How will the army be destroyed? God will use four means to bring on its demise: earthquake; self-destruction; pestilence (disease); and the Lord will rain fire and brimstone on them (Ezek. 39:4, 20-22). Some see the fire and brimstone as being a nuclear explosion, but this is impossible since it would mean destruction of all Israel. The destruction of this army will be so vast that it will take seven months to bury the dead (Ezek. 39:12, 14).

Joel promised Judah that she would not have to lift a finger to defend herself; God would remove the enemy (v. 20). The same will be true when the Russian confederacy descends on Israel in the latter days. God will completely destroy the army sent into the Middle East (Ezek. 39:2-4, 6, 11).

PROTECTED BY THE LORD (v. 19)

God told Judah that He would not only remove the prophesied plague and deliver them from impending destruction, but He would *no more* make them a reproach among the nations (v. 19). This last statement has not been fulfilled as yet, for Israel is still a reproach among the nations. The Jew has been hated and discriminated against by many nations even before Joel's time to the present day.

On November 10, 1975, the United Nations General Assembly passed a resolution vilifying the Zionist Movement as "a form of racism or racial discrimination," on a 72 to 35 vote with 32 abstentions and 3 absences. [3]

The United States Ambassador, Daniel Moynihan, called the resolution an "obscene act." [4] He went on to say, "It was not Zionism that was condemned at the United Nations on Friday, it was Israel."

When will Israel's reproach from among the nations be removed? The reproach will be removed when Christ returns to set up the Millennial Kingdom on earth.

PROSPERITY FROM THE LORD (vv. 19, 21-27)

Since God heard the repentant cry of Judah, removed the curse and brought healing to the land, Joel calls upon all of creation to replace their fear with gladness and rejoicing (vv. 21, 23).

Comparing this section with the prophecies given in chapters one and two, a number of contrasts can be seen. First, the *denuded land* (1:17-20) will break forth in gladness and joy (2:21) when new life springs forth because of the former and latter rain (2:23). Second, animals will not have to fear for their survival because the barren pastures (1:19-20) will spring forth in greenness (2:22); withered trees and vines (1:12) will produce an abundance of fruit (2:22). Third, man who was called to weep, wail, lament and be ashamed will be glad and rejoice (v. 23) over the lifting of the curse and renewal of the land.

This is a foretaste of what Israel will experience during the Millennial Kingdom. When Christ returns, He shall give to the *children of Zion* (v. 23), ". . . beauty for ashes, the oil of joy for mourning, the garment of praise for the spirit of heaviness . . ." (Isa. 61:3). Jerusalem will be a place of rejoicing, and the voice of weeping and crying will be removed (Isa. 65:18-19).

The *animal kingdom* will be at peace, for "The wolf and the lamb shall feed together, and the lion shall eat straw like the bullock . . . They shall not hurt nor destroy . . ." (Isa. 65:25). Notice, all of the animal kingdom is to be changed except the serpent who caused Eve to sin. He will still crawl upon his belly obtaining his food from the dust of the earth (Isa.

65:25).

Israel will rejoice because God has given her "the former rain moderately . . . and the latter rain in the first month" (v. 23). This phrase has been debated for centuries as to its meaning — whether it should be interpreted spiritually or physically in context.

Some want to interpret the passage *spiritually* since the phrase "former rain [lit., *a teacher*] moderately [lit., *unto righteousness*]" can be translated *a teacher of righteousness.* Many rabbis in times past interpreted this phrase in reference to the Messiah, for He is a teacher come from God to show the way of righteousness. Other rabbis see the phrase as referring to any prophet who brings righteous instruction. Still others interpret the words *rain for righteousness* as a sign that God has restored Judah to a position of righteousness.

Although all of the above is true, it seems best to interpret the section as having reference to *physical* rain since the context bears this out. In context, the phrase "former rain moderately" is better interpreted *to rain in right measure.* The rain will be of great blessing to Israel during the Kingdom Age because the Lord will send it in the right amount at the proper time. The "former rain" comes in abundance during the autumn (October) to prepare the land for sowing, and the "latter rain" comes in the spring (April) just before the harvest. By providing the rain in right measure, the Lord is assuring Israel of her right relationship with Him during the Millennium (Lev. 26:3-4; Dt. 11:13-15).

To the cynic who said, "Where is their God?" (v. 17), God answers, "And I will restore to you the years that the locusts hath eaten . . ." (v. 25). Notice, Joel does not say year, but "years" which the locust have eaten. The reference is not to swarms of locusts invading Judah for several years in succession, but to the crop lost for a number of years due to the devastation of the land by the locust plague.

The effects of restoration to both people and land are that they have great abundance of grain, wine and oil (v. 19); their "floors shall be full of wheat, and the vats shall overflow with wine and oil" (v. 24). Amos, echoing this passage said, "Behold, the days come, saith the Lord, that the plowman shall overtake the reaper, and the treader of grapes him that soweth seed..." (Amos 9:13). What a contrast to the earlier prophecy of desolation (1:10-12)!

Judah's renewed prosperity will produce inner satisfaction and outward praise (v. 26) unto their God who will again prove Himself to be gracious, merciful and loving to a repentant people. Joel reminds the people that God has dealt with them "wondrously" (v. 26); that is, He worked in a miraculous way in bringing restoration to both Judah and the land.

Through this renewal experience, both Judah and the surrounding nations will learn a number of lessons. First, Israel is God's *people* (v. 27). Seeing their helpless situations, He has pity (v. 18) on them. Second, God is *present* with His people (v. 27) and will not forsake them in times of disobedience. Third, God *protects* Israel from those bent on her destruction. God will destroy the "northern army" (v. 20) who will come in the latter days. Fourth, God provides *prosperity* for a people who walk before Him in righteousness (vv. 19, 23-24) before the nations of the world by trusting in Him, the true and living God.

Israel's experience typifies the life of many Christians today. They are the people of God, having trusted Christ as their Savior. God's presence indwells them through the ministry of the Holy Spirit. He protects them from the onslaughts of Satan who is bent on their destruction. Yet, their lives lack spiritual prosperity, for sin has severed their fellowship in Christ.

Like Israel, they need to turn from sin with a repentant heart if God is to show pity and provide pardon. Sad to say, many will not turn, but will wander in the wilderness of sin for years, spiritually blind and bankrupt.

Yet, God promises spiritual intervention if they turn to Him. He will bring the former and latter rain of spiritual renewal, restoring the years which the locust of sin have destroyed.

What pleasant words are they, "... restore to you the years that the locust hath eaten ..." (v. 25). True, years of sin leave their mark on mind and body. True, years of sin are unredeemable. But the repentant Christian can experience a new beginning and enjoy the fullness of spiritual blessing in each fresh tomorrow.

For those who return, God promises to take away the shame of sin. Why delay, come today!

JOEL 2:28-32

And it shall come to pass afterward, that I will pour out my Spirit upon all flesh; and your sons and your daughters shall prophesy, your old men shall dream dreams, your young men shall see visions; And, also, upon the servants and upon the handmaids in those days will I pour out my Spirit. And I will show wonders in the heavens and in the earth: blood, and fire, and pillars of smoke. The sun shall be turned into darkness, and the moon into blood, before the great and terrible day of the Lord come. And it shall come to pass that whosoever shall call on the name of the Lord shall be delivered; for in Mount Zion and in Jerusalem shall be deliverance, as the Lord hath said, and in the remnant whom the Lord shall call.

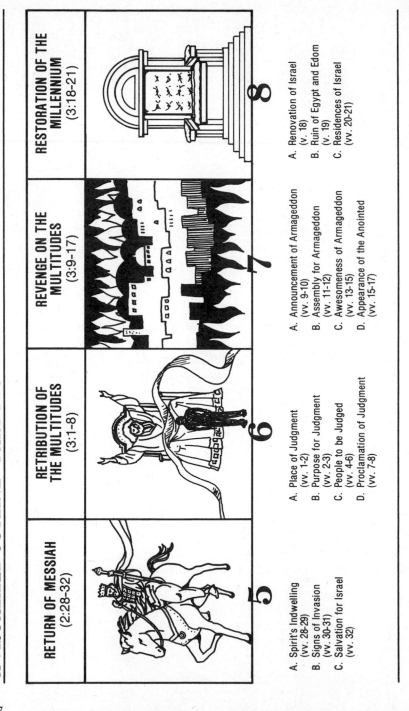

A VISUALIZED OUTLINE - PART TWO

RETURN OF MESSIAH (2:28-32)	RETRIBUTION OF THE MULTITUDES (3:1-8)	REVENGE ON THE MULTITUDES (3:9-17)	RESTORATION OF THE MILLENNIUM (3:18-21)
5	**6**	**7**	**8**
A. Spirit's Indwelling (vv. 28-29) B. Signs of Invasion (vv. 30-31) C. Salvation for Israel (vv. 32)	A. Place of Judgment (vv. 1-2) B. Purpose for Judgment (vv. 2-3) C. People to be Judged (vv. 4-6) D. Proclamation of Judgment (vv. 7-8)	A. Announcement of Armageddon (vv. 9-10) B. Assembly for Armageddon (vv. 11-12) C. Awesomeness of Armageddon (vv. 13-15) D. Appearance of the Anointed (vv. 15-17)	A. Renovation of Israel (v. 18) B. Ruin of Egypt and Edom (v. 19) C. Residences of Israel (vv. 20-21)

5

THE DAY OF THE LORD: RETURN OF THE MESSIAH

Joel 2:28-32

The cry of this age is peace, peace, peace! Men are looking for peace and security. They want job security, health security and life security — a time when war will cease and universal peace will prevail forever.

God has promised a golden age of peace, a time when war, famine, flood and disease will cease. This age is called the Millennium by theologians. The term "Millennium" is not found in the Bible, but comes from two Latin words, *mille (thousand)* and *annum (year),* having reference to the thousand-year reign of Christ. His reign is clearly taught in Scripture, "Blessed and holy is he that hath part in the first resurrection . . . they shall be priests of God and of Christ, and shall *reign with him a thousand years*" (Rev. 20:6).

With a sweep of the pen Joel transports the reader to the time of Christ's Second Coming, and enumerates many of the spiritual blessings to be experienced by all believers. But how does the reader know this passage projects him into the Kingdom Age? First, Joel indicates it with the words, "it shall come to pass *afterward*" (v. 28). *Afterward* refers to the time of the Millennium. This is beautifully illustrated in Hosea 3:1-5. Hosea mentions Israel's past (vv. 1-2); her present (vv. 3-4); and links the Kingdom Age to what has been mentioned

before by using the word "Afterward" (v. 5). Second, the
spiritual events of this section transcend Joel's day and will
only be fulfilled during the second advent of Christ.

In the Hebrew Bible, verses 28-32 comprise a separate
chapter (Joel 3) which describes three great spiritual experi-
ences to be enjoyed by Israel: the coming of the Lord;
salvation to the nation; and the permanent indwelling and
filling of the Holy Spirit.

SIGNS BEFORE INVASION (vv. 30-31)

Joel mentions that the Lord's coming will be preceded by
certain signs, "And I will show wonders in the heavens and in
the earth" (v. 30). The wonders in the earth are blood, fire
and smoke (v. 30). How is one to interpret such an awesome
sight painted by Joel?

The wonders in *earth* are a manifestation of God's judgment on ungodly men at the pouring out of the seal, trumpet
and bowl judgments. First, *blood* will be profusely poured out
during the Tribulation. When the fourth seal judgment is
opened, one-fourth of the world's population will be killed
(Rev. 6:8). The trumpet judgment will destroy a third of both
sea and human life (Rev. 8:9; 9:15). During the bowl
judgments the remaining sea will become like the blood of a
dead man causing the demise of all sea creatures (Rev.
16:3). At the campaign of Armageddon blood will reach to the
horse bridles for a distance of 200 miles in circumference
(Rev. 14:20).

Second, *fire* will devastate the earth in the Tribulation.
During the trumpet judgment a censer of fire will be flung to
earth burning a third of all vegetation (Rev. 8:5, 7; cp. 8:8,
10). The fourth bowl judgment will produce an unbearable
scorching of men with fire (Rev. 16:8).

Third, fire will produce *smoke* which is mentioned in many
of the judgments. The most graphic picture of smoke is
described with the fifth trumpet judgment. When the bottomless pit is opened, out will emerge smoke so dense that it will
darken the atmosphere blotting out the light of day (Rev.

9:2). Emerging from the smoke will come an unspeakable judgment of demonic spirits possessing a strange body which will be used to torment the unsaved earth (Rev. 9:5-10).

The wonders in *the heavens* will affect both the sun and moon (v. 31). Jesus predicted that there will be signs in the heavens just prior to His return; both sun and moon will be darkened and the stars will fall from the heavens (Mt. 24:29).

Today there is much confusion over the Second Coming of Christ. Many call the Rapture of the Church the Second Coming, but it is not! The Rapture will take place seven years prior to the Second Coming, when the dead and alive in Christ rise to meet Him in the air (1 Th. 4:13-17).

The Second Coming may be defined as the visible return of Christ in brilliant glory (with angels and the Church) at the end of the Tribulation to reign on earth for a thousand years. There are 333 prophecies which speak of Christ's coming; only 109 mention the first advent, but twice as many (224) tell of His Second Coming.

Christ's Second Coming is a major theme, not only in the Old Testament, but in the New Testament as well. Four key words are used in the New Testament to describe His coming. The Lord's return is called a *coming* (Gr., Erchomai). Although Christ had to leave His disciples, He promised to "come again" and receive them unto Himself (Jn. 14:3). His coming will be sudden (Mt. 24:39, 42-44, 48, 50), with power and great glory at the end of the Tribulation (Mt. 24:29-30).

Christ's return is called a *revelation* (Gr., Apokalupsis), or an unveiling. His presence will be suddenly unveiled as the clouds part and He descends from Heaven to take vengeance upon the enemies of Israel (2 Th. 1:7-8, 10).

Scripture presents Christ's return as a *manifestation* or an *appearing* (Gr., Epiphaneia), more literally, *a shining forth.* The word was used in the Grecian-Roman period of the first century to describe the appearance of their gods to men, or the sudden appearance of an enemy arrayed in battle dress. It describes Christ's coming (2 Tim. 1:10) as a sudden "appearing" (Ti. 2:13) with great power and "brightness" (2

Th. 2:8) to destroy His enemies.

Last, Christ's coming is mentioned as a *presence* (Gr., parousia). The word is used in reference to the arrival of a king on his royal visit. Again, His presence (translated *coming*) will be a sudden, unexpected arrival (Mt. 24:37-39), as the KING OF KINGS AND LORD OF LORDS (Rev. 19:16) to be the ruler of earth.

For what purpose will He return? He will come back to defeat Israel's enemies (Zech. 14:12-13; Rev. 19:19-21); liberate the world from Satan's control (2 Th. 2:8-9); bring salvation to the Jewish people (Rom. 11:26); judge the nations and give the Kingdom to the redeemed of all ages (Mt. 25:31-46); set up a kingdom of peace on earth centered in Israel (Mic. 4:3-5); and deliver all of creation from the curse brought on through man's sin (Rom. 8:19-22).

SALVATION FOR ISRAEL (v. 32)

Knowing the horrors of the Great Tribulation, will any escape the terrible *day of the Lord?* Yes, a "remnant whom the Lord shall call" (v. 32) will be saved to enter the Kingdom. Notice, only a remnant out of the thousands shall be saved. Zechariah states that two-thirds of the Jewish population will be killed during the Tribulation. The one third that survives will be the remnant who call upon the Lord (Zech. 13:8-9). The spared remnant will be Jewish people "who keep the commandments of God, and have the testimony of Jesus Christ" (Rev. 12:17). God will supernaturally provide a place of protection for them in the wilderness during the last three and one-half years of the Tribulation (Rev. 12:16). Before Israel went into the land of Canaan, Moses predicted that a remnant who called on the Lord would be saved during the Tribulation (Dt. 4:30-31). So complete is every detail of God's prophetic Word!

How will salvation come to this remnant? After the Lord destroys the armies who converge upon Jerusalem, He will set His feet upon the Mount of Olives which will immediately split apart forming a massive valley before the East Gate of Jerusalem (Zech. 14:4). Upon Christ's arrival the Jewish people, who have had a veil over their eyes for centuries (2 Cor. 3:14-16), will have it lifted to see that He is the true Messiah. Repentance will take place as never before in Israel. Zechariah wrote, ". . . and they shall look upon me whom they have pierced, and they shall mourn for him, as one mourneth for his only son, and shall be in bitterness for him, as one that is in bitterness for his firstborn" (Zech. 12:10). This is a fulfillment of Paul's prophecy, ". . . all Israel shall be saved; as it is written, There shall come out of Zion the Deliverer, and shall turn away ungodliness from Jacob" (Rom. 11:26). Upon their repentance, God will take away the sin of His people (Ezek. 36:25; 37:23) by means of Jesus' blood, which is the fountain for their cleansing (Zech. 13:1), and will bring to fruition the provisions prophesied in the New Covenant centuries ago (Ezek. 36:26-27; Jer. 31:31-34).

For centuries Jewish people have been buried on the Mount of Olives facing the Temple mount in the hope that they will be resurrected to enter Jerusalem with the Messiah. Sad to say, this will not be their destiny unless they received Jesus as Messiah in this life.

THE SPIRIT'S INDWELLING (vv. 28-29)

Zechariah said that the Spirit of God will be poured out on the house of David and Jerusalem (Zech. 12:10) at Christ's return. Joel, being more inclusive, states that the Holy Spirit will be poured out on "all flesh" (v. 28). The interpretation of these verses has been debated for centuries, since Peter used them during his first sermon to the Jewish people gathered for the Feast of Pentecost.

The question is asked, *Were these verses fulfilled completely, partly or not at all on the day of Pentecost?* Today the following positions are held by Bible scholars concerning the interpretation of Acts 2:16-21:

Historical View
Joel's prophecy was fulfilled during the writing of his book.

Fulfillment View
Joel's prophecy was fulfilled on the day of Pentecost.

Typical View
Joel's prophecy was fulfilled in type on the day of Pentecost, but awaits greater fulfillment during the Millennium.

Perpetual View
Joel's prophecy was fulfilled on the day of Pentecost and will continue to be fulfilled through the Church Age and Millennium.

Eschatological View
Joel's prophecy was not fulfilled on the day of Pentecost, nor in the Church Age, but awaits fulfillment at the Second Coming of Christ. [1]

Many believers teach view number four, the perpetual fulfillment of Joel's prophecy from the day of Pentecost onward. They reason, *Did not Peter say, "But this is that which was spoken through the prophet, Joel" (Acts 2:16), thus a fulfillment of Joel's prophecy!* But is Peter saying that Joel's prophecy was *fulfilled* at Pentecost? A closer examination of Peter's exact words will indicate that he *did not* say Joel's prophecy was fulfilled on the day of Pentecost. In fact, he never used the word "fulfilled" or any other synonym to suggest fulfillment.

Then what is Peter saying? The context shows that some Jews were mocking the apostles (who had spoken to the people in their own languages), supposing that they were drunk at nine o'clock in the morning (Acts 2:1-15). In order to counter the Jewish mockers, Peter says, *"this is that"* (Acts 2:16), or in essence, stop your mocking for *this is similar* to what Joel said would happen when God pours His Spirit on all flesh prior to the establishment of the Kingdom Age. If this were a fulfillment of Joel's prophecy, Peter would have said, "this is a fulfillment." Although many Christians believe Acts 2:16-21 is a fulfillment of Joel's prophecy, Peter is cautious to omit the word *fulfillment.*

There is a second reason why Joel's prophecy was not fulfilled at Pentecost. Joel said God would pour His Spirit out on *"all flesh"* (v. 28). At Pentecost God did not pour His Spirit on all flesh, but on a select group of people, and likewise today. God will not pour out His Spirit on all flesh until the Kingdom Age.

Another reason why Joel's prophecy was not fulfilled on the day of Pentecost is clearly seen in Acts 2:17-21. Peter went on to quote, "And I will show wonders in heaven above, and signs in earth beneath: blood, and fire, and vapor of smoke. The sun shall be turned into darkness, and the moon into blood, before that great and notable day of the Lord come" (Acts 2:19-20; cp. Joel 2:30-31). All who know what happened on the day of Pentecost will agree that these prophecies were not fulfilled. Scripture very distinctly presents that these prophecies are to be fulfilled in "the great and the terrible day of the Lord" (v. 31) at the end of the Tribulation period.

The Holy Spirit will be manifested in all His fullness during the Millennial Kingdom, much greater than during any period in history. It will be the Spirit's ministry to restrain *sin.* There will be no spiritual conflict since demonic activity is nonexistent, for Satan is bound in the bottomless pit (Rev. 20:1-3), and Christ is suppressing evil by ruling with a rod of iron (Rev. 19:15). True, there will be people born during the Kingdom Age with a sinful nature, who will try to manifest their wickedness (Isa. 65:20), but the Holy Spirit will restrain them.

It will be the Spirit's ministry to convict people of their need for *salvation.* Though freed from the oppressive domination of Satanic power, men will still need to receive Christ. Those born during the Kingdom Age will be led to Christ by the Holy Spirit like their parents before them (Ezek. 36:25-31; Jer. 31:31-34; Zech. 14:16; Isa. 60:3-12).

It will be the Spirit's ministry to completely control every aspect of the *saint's* life during the Millennium. The Lord says, "And I will put my Spirit within you, and cause you to walk in my statutes, and ye shall keep mine ordinances, and do them" (Ezek. 36:27). No longer will the believer quench or grieve the Holy Spirit as in the Church Age, but spiritual unity, as well as the fruit of the Spirit, will be perfectly manifested in every aspect of the believer's life and fellowship. This will produce a righteous life, inner joy and peace, which flows out in worship and praise to the Lord.

It will be the Spirit's ministry to rest upon the *Savior* in His sevenfold fullness. The Spirit gives Christ quick understanding with which to righteously judge and rule upon the earth (Isa. 11:2-5).

John W. Peterson picked up the expectant joy that awaits every believer who is anticipating the soon return of the Lord when he wrote, "Maybe morning, maybe noon, maybe evening and maybe soon! . . . O what a wonderful day it will be — Jesus is coming again!" Yes, Jesus is coming again for those who know Him, and what a day of rejoicing it will be. But He comes in judgment for those who are lost. The first phrase of this hymn, "Marvelous message we bring," summons every Christian to a responsibility for heralding the warning to those who are lost, for the only guarantee man has for peace and security in this life and the one to come is salvation in Christ! "Coming again, coming again . . . maybe soon." Let us be about the Father's business.

JOEL 3:1-8

For, behold, in those days, and in that time, when I shall bring again the captivity of Judah and Jerusalem, I will also gather all nations, and will bring them down into the Valley of Jehoshaphat, and will judge them there for my people and for my heritage, Israel, whom they have scattered among the nations, and parted my land. And they have cast lots for my people, and have given a boy for an harlot, and sold a girl for wine, that they might drink. Yea, and what have ye to do with me, O Tyre, and Sidon, and all the coasts of Philistia? Will ye render me a recompense? And if ye recompense me, swiftly and speedily will I return your recompense upon your own head, Because ye have taken my silver and my gold, and have carried into your temples my precious things. The children also of Judah, and the children of Jerusalem, have ye sold unto the Grecians, that ye might remove them far from their border. Behold, I will raise them out of the place to which ye have sold them, and will return your recompense upon your own head. And I will sell your sons and your daughters into the hand of the children of Judah, and they shall sell them to the men of Sheba, to a people far off; for the Lord hath spoken it.

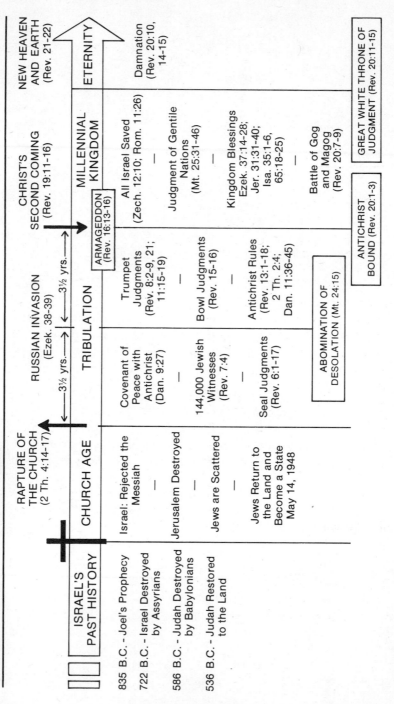

ISRAEL THROUGH THE AGES

ISRAEL'S PAST HISTORY	CHURCH AGE	TRIBULATION	MILLENNIAL KINGDOM	ETERNITY
		RUSSIAN INVASION (Ezek. 38-39)		NEW HEAVEN AND EARTH (Rev. 21-22)
	RAPTURE OF THE CHURCH (2 Th. 4:14-17)	←3½ yrs.→ ←3½ yrs.→ ARMAGEDDON (Rev. 16:13-16)	CHRIST'S SECOND COMING (Rev. 19:11-16)	

835 B.C. - Joel's Prophecy

722 B.C. - Israel Destroyed by Assyrians

586 B.C. - Judah Destroyed by Babylonians

536 B.C. - Judah Restored to the Land

Israel: Rejected the Messiah

Jerusalem Destroyed

Jews are Scattered

Jews Return to the Land and Become a State May 14, 1948

Covenant of Peace with Antichrist (Dan. 9:27)

144,000 Jewish Witnesses (Rev. 7:4)

Seal Judgments (Rev. 6:1-17)

Trumpet Judgments (Rev. 8:2-9, 21; 11:15-19)

Bowl Judgments (Rev. 15-16)

Antichrist Rules (Rev. 13:1-18; 2 Th. 2:4; Dan. 11:36-45)

All Israel Saved (Zech. 12:10; Rom. 11:26)

Judgment of Gentile Nations (Mt. 25:31-46)

Kingdom Blessings Ezek. 37:14-28; Jer. 31:31-40; Isa. 35:1-6; 65:18-25)

Battle of Gog and Magog (Rev. 20:7-9)

Damnation (Rev. 20:10, 14-15)

ABOMINATION OF DESOLATION (Mt. 24:15)

ANTICHRIST BOUND (Rev. 20:1-3)

GREAT WHITE THRONE OF JUDGMENT (Rev. 20:11-15)

6

THE DAY OF THE LORD: RETRIBUTION ON THE MULTITUDES

Joel 3:1-8

The struggles and sufferings of Israel are well documented from Egyptian slavery to the Roman destruction of Jerusalem. Like an echo, the Diaspora Jew would face nineteen more centuries of anguish as the shadow of persecution dogged their every footstep throughout the world. They would experience the fire of the Spanish Inquisition, the stench of Vienna's ghetto, the poverty of Poland's peasantry, the sword of Russian pogroms and the horrible heel of Nazi annihilation.

Arising from the ashes of despair comes the cry, *Where was God in defense of His people?* He was there, not taken by surprise at the cruelty perpetrated against His chosen, but silently waiting for the fulfillment of His Word predicted centuries earlier, for Moses had predicted in the Law that Israel's disobedience would produce God's discipline (Lev. 26; Dt. 4:25-31; 28:15-68).

Sad to say, the discipline is not finished. Israel is yet to face her greatest holocaust known as "Jacob's trouble" (Jer. 30:7), a time of unprecedented persecution when, once again, the nations of the world will converge upon Israel (Zech. 14:2).

Is there any justice? Will the Jew be vindicated for the

many centuries of suffering? Yes, Scripture is clear, the
nations will pay for their dastardly deeds against this
downtrodden people!

In chapter three the reader is ushered into Messiah's
courtroom to witness the execution of His judgment upon the
Gentiles for their treatment of Israel. Joel, like many prophets, does not always follow the chronological order of
prophetic events. In this section he presents the judgment of
the nations (vv. 1-8) before the battle of Armageddon (vv. 9-
17). Why? Because the Gentiles' horrible treatment of Israel
through the centuries is the purpose for His judgment on
them.

PLACE OF JUDGMENT (vv. 1-2)

Joel introduces chapter three with the words, "For,
behold" (v. 1), drawing the reader's attention to what is
about to unfold as he explains in detail the action taken by the
Lord at His return to set up the Kingdom. First, God will "...
bring again the captivity of Judah and Jerusalem" (v. 1), or,
more literally, cause their captivity and persecution to cease.
Not only will He cause their captivity to cease, but He will
regather the Diaspora Jew back to the land so the twelve
tribes can be one people in the land (Jer. 23:1-8; Ezek. 37:15-
22).

God will not only gather Israel to the land, but He will "...
gather all nations . . . into the Valley of Jehoshaphat" (v. 2) for
the purpose of judgment.

Where is the Valley of Jehoshaphat? Some say it is the
Beracah Valley, so named because Jehoshaphat defeated
the Moabites and Ammonites in this area, gaining a great
victory (2 Chr. 20:20-28). But this valley is not in the proper
location for the judgment of the Lord. Others believe
Jehoshaphat's valley is located between Jerusalem and the
Mount of Olives, which has been called the Kidron Valley
since the fourth century (named after a small river which runs
through it during the rainy season). Since the Mount of
Olives will be split forming a massive valley before Jerusalem

(Zech. 14:4), this is probably the place where Christ will judge the nations. Because Jehoshaphat means *Jehovah judges,* the valley has taken on this name; thus, a play on words, God's judgment takes place in the valley of God, the Judge.

What judgment is this? This is when God will judge the Gentile nations who have survived the Great Tribulation (Mt. 25:31-46) and will take place on earth after the Second Coming of the Lord. One should not confuse this with the Great White Throne Judgment which will take place after the Millennial Kingdom.

What is meant by judgment of the nations? The word "nation" (Gr., ethnos) refers to the judgment of individual Gentiles within the country, not the judgment of whole nations. The following reasons bear this out. First, the message of salvation presented in the Tribulation calls for an individual acceptance, not a national one. Second, there is no record in Scripture that whole Gentile nations will accept the preaching of the 144,000 Jewish witnesses. Third, in all the judgments presented in Scripture, it is the individual, not the nation, who is judged. Fourth, the parables on judgment presented by Christ (Mt. 13:30, 47-50) are on individuals. Fifth, the term *nation* is used in other portions of the New Testament with reference to individuals (Mt. 6:31-32; 12:21; 20:19; 28:19; Acts 11:18; 15:3; 26:20).

PEOPLE TO BE JUDGED (vv. 4-6)

Although God will judge all nations equally, the Phoenicians (Tyre and Sidon) and Philistines (v. 4) are set forth as examples because of their harsh treatment against Israel.

Lands belonging to the Phoenicians and Philistines were given to Israel as an inheritance by God (Josh. 13:1-7). Israel was to drive these people from the land but failed to do so in obedience to God's command (Jud. 1:21-36). Thus, both peoples became a thorn in Israel's side for centuries (Jud. 2:1-6). The Philistines were fierce enemies of Israel from Samson's day until the middle of David's reign and still warred against Israel until the days of Joel.

The last recorded invasion by the Philistines was against King Jehoram and his family resulting in their plunder and destruction; only Jehoahaz, the youngest son of Jehoram, survived (2 Chr. 21:16-17).

The Philistines deserve strong judgment not only for destroying King Jehoram and his family but for taking their treasures. Notice, God said they did not take Jehoram's treasures, but, ". . . ye have taken *my* silver and *my* gold, and . . . *my* precious things" (v. 5; cp. Hos. 2:8; Hag. 2:8). What Judah owns, God owns! They have doubly insulted God. Not only did they carry away His possessions, but they dedicated these treasures to their lifeless idols in worship (v. 5).

Next, God will judge the Phoenicians and Philistines for selling the children of Judah into slavery (v. 6). The Phoenicians were noted men stealers who trafficked heavily in the slave trade with Greece, Tubal and Meshech (Ezek. 27:13). Such acts were forbidden by a "brotherly covenant" (Amos 1:6, 9) made between Solomon and Tyre's King Hiram.

Greeks sold young men and women from their country to Egypt and Persia. At its zenith, Greece had acquired some 1,330,000 slaves. It has been said that 10,000 slaves per day were sold at Delos. [1]

By removing Jews "far from their border" (v. 6), the Philistines weakened Judah which eventually resulted in their victory over the land.

God's attitude toward Phoenicia and the Philistines is harsh. He asked them two questions in verse four. First, ". . . what have ye to do with me . . . ?" (literally, *What are ye to me?*). He is saying, *What have we in common?* The answer is, Nothing! Second, "Will ye render me a recompense?" That is, do they realize that by injuring His people they injure Him. God will retaliate "swiftly and speedily" (v. 4) with the same treatment poured out upon the heads of Judah's enemies. History is replete with incidents of how swiftly God will judge those who touch the Jew. After the Tribulation, God will bring swift judgment upon Israel's enemies.

PURPOSE FOR JUDGMENT (vv. 2-3)

God will judge the Gentile nations for the way they have treated the Jew, His "people and . . . heritage" (v. 2). First, they "scattered [them] among the nations" (v. 2). Although the Assyrians and Babylonians did not scatter the nation of Israel, they devastated the people. Assyria destroyed the ten tribes of Israel in 722 B.C., and the Babylonians leveled Judah in 586 B.C. It was not until the Romans destroyed Jerusalem (A.D. 70) that the Jew was scattered across the earth to suffer as no other people in human history.

Second, not only did the nations scatter the people, but God said they "parted my land" (v. 2). For nineteen centuries the land was downtrodden, divided and desolate, being occupied during this period by some fourteen various powers at one time or another.

Third, the Gentiles will be judged for selling the sons and daughters of Judah into slavery (vv. 3, 6). A boy was given into slavery as payment for one night with a prostitute, and a girl turned over for a meager bottle of wine (v. 3). After destroying Jerusalem, the Romans disposed of Jews in the following way. The tallest and most beautiful were chosen out, marched back to Rome, and then paraded before the people in triumph. Those above seventeen years of age were sold into Egyptian slavery to work in the mines.[2] Those under seventeen were simply sold among the nations to the highest bidder. The slave markets were so glutted with Jewish slaves that enough buyers could not be found.

Israel will once again feel the iron heel of Gentile hatred and persecution during the Tribulation. The Antichrist will turn on the Jews, break the covenant of peace made with them (Dan. 9:27), and kill all who will not worship him as God (Mt. 24:15-22; Rev. 12:13-17; 13:15). With the Tribulation drawing to a close, the nations of the world converge upon Israel to do battle, resulting in two-thirds of the Jewish population being killed (Zech. 13:8) and one-half of Jerusalem taken captive (Zech. 14:2).

Christ will judge the nations at His return on the basis of how they treated His "brethren" (Mt. 25:40). Who are the brethren mentioned in Matthew 25? It cannot be the Church, for it will be raptured before the Tribulation begins. It must be referring to His "brethren," the Jew.

By what standard will the Gentiles be judged? It seems as if they will be judged according to their works (Mt. 25:42-45), and not on the basis of whether they have salvation. But this is not the case. Man is never saved by works but on his acceptance of Jesus Christ. The ones judged are described as being cursed, having their destiny sealed to the Lake of Fire (Mt. 25:41, 46). A second group described as "righteous" (Mt. 25:37) will help the suffering Jewish remnant during the Tribulation by *feeding, clothing, housing* and *visiting imprisoned Jewish brethren* (Mt. 25:35-40).

The Gentiles are considered righteous or cursed on the basis of whether they received or rejected the gospel of the Kingdom (Mt. 24:14). In accepting the message, they would have received the messengers as well. Thus, they show their faith by feeding, clothing, housing and visiting the Jewish brethren imprisoned for their faith. Rahab is a classic illustration of how one shows faith in the God of Israel by helping the Jewish spies escape from Jericho (Josh. 2; Heb. 11:31). When God judges the Gentiles, all He will need to examine is the person's treatment of Jewish believers to know whether the individual has accepted Christ.

PROCLAMATION OF JUDGMENT (vv. 7-8)

Joel declares that God will bring retribution on Phoenicia and the Philistines for their harsh treatment toward the Jews.

Tyre's destruction is graphically predicted by Ezekiel (Ezek. 26-28). Although it would take Nebuchadnezzar thirteen years (585-573) to besiege Tyre, he completely destroyed and enslaved this people (Ezek. 26:7-14).

A remnant of Tyre escaped to a small island offshore, and there they rebuilt their city. For two hundred and forty years they thrived until Alexander the Great laid siege to the island city. He tried for seven months to conquer the impregnable city and finally succeeded after building a causeway to it from ruins off the mainland in 332 B.C. Although Ezekiel's prophecy was literally fulfilled (Ezek. 27:32), Tyre was rebuilt (Mt. 15:21-28; Acts 21:3-6) only to be destroyed by the Moslems in A.D. 1291. Today the area is inhabited by a few thousand people, but the city remains in ruins as prophesied (Ezek. 26:14). Sidon, the sister city (Ezek. 28:21-28), and the Philistines (Isa. 14:28-31; Ezek. 25:15-17) suffered the same fate as Tyre.

Joel prophesied that these people would be sold to Israel, who in turn sold them to the Sabeans (vv. 7-8), a people in southwest Arabia (Jer. 6:20; Ezek. 27:22; 38:13). God used the Greek (Alexander the Great), to whom Tyre sold Jewish slaves, to destroy and sell them into slavery.

The same fate that befell the Phoenicians and Philistines will come upon all nations when God judges them in Jehoshaphat's valley. Two destinies are described in Matthew 25 for those who survive the Tribulation. The "righteous," designated as sheep, will be put on the Lord's right hand to enter into the Kingdom prepared for them from the foundation of the world (Mt. 25:33-34). But the "unrighteous," those designated as goats, will be put on the left hand, judged and consigned to the ". . . everlasting fire, prepared for the devil and his angels" (Mt. 25:33, 41).

God said about Judah, ". . . for he that toucheth you toucheth the apple of his eye" (Zech. 2:8). The term "apple of his eye" is used to speak of the *aperture* (literally, the gate) of the eye, known as the pupil. When an individual looks into the eye of another, he sees a reflected image of himself from the person's pupil. Israel is the *little man* reflected from the pupil of God's eye. The Jew is so precious to God that He protects him as He would His own eye. When the Jew is afflicted, God feels it as if it happened to Him.

America has experienced unprecedented peace, power and prosperity because it has allowed the Jew to coexist on its shores in peace. Pray that this nation continues to have a heartbeat for Israel as she struggles against the suppressing aggressors who desire to snuff out her life. If the nation's attitude is less toward the Jew, it will see reflected back from God's eye the ugly image of its own prejudice and God's divine displeasure.

Let us all purpose to treat Israel, the apple of God's eye, with respect and love. Remember the eternal principle given in an unconditional covenant to Abraham, "And I will bless them that bless thee [the Jew], and curse him that curseth thee [the Jew]: and in thee [the Jew] shall all families of the earth be blessed" (Gen. 12:3). Both secular and biblical history have proven this to be true for some 4,000 years.

JOEL 3:9-17

Proclaim this among the nations, Prepare war, wake up the mighty men, let all the men of war draw near; let them come up; Beat your plowshares into swords, and your pruning hooks into spears; let the weak say, I am strong. Assemble yourselves, and come, all ye nations, and gather yourselves together round about; there cause thy mighty ones to come down, O Lord. Let the nations be wakened, and come up to the Valley of Jehoshaphat; for there will I sit to judge all the nations round about. Put in the sickle; for the harvest is ripe; come, get down; for the press is full, the vats overflow; for their wickedness is great. Multitudes, multitudes in the valley of decision; for the day of the Lord is near in the valley of decision. The sun and the moon shall be darkened, and the stars shall withdraw their shining. The Lord also shall roar out of Zion, and utter his voice from Jerusalem, and the heavens and the earth shall shake; but the Lord will be the hope of his people, and the strength of the children of Israel. So shall ye know that I am the Lord, your God, dwelling in Zion, my holy mountain; then shall Jerusalem be holy, and there shall no strangers pass through her any more.

COMBATANTS OF ARMAGEDDON

EUROPE (10 – Nation United States of Europe)
Antichrist

CHINA
Kings of the east

King of
the north

ISRAEL

EGYPT
King of the south

7

THE DAY OF THE LORD: REVENGE ON THE MULTITUDES

Joel 3:9-17

An estimated 100 million Americans watched ABC's special, "The Day After." The nation saw Lawrence, Kansas atomized before their eyes. Young and old were impacted by the television special, leaving many in a state of fear and uncertainty concerning their survival if a nuclear bomb were dropped.

Many peace movements hyped the television special, using it as a platform for their nuclear weapon freeze program or total disarmament. Supporters of these movements believe that a nuclear disaster would not only bring massive destruction, but annihilate life on this planet.

On the other hand, some political leaders are calling for a nuclear buildup in order to gain parity with the Soviet Union, hoping to assure world peace. They believe that strong superpowers will not engage each other for fear of nuclear annihilation.

Some evangelists are heralding that Armageddon is at hand. They preach that a nuclear holocaust will emerge in the Middle East precipitated by a clash of superpowers around the nation of Israel.

Will Armageddon be a nuclear holocaust resulting in the annihilation of life on this planet? Before answering this question, it must be determined how the term *Armageddon* is used in Scripture.

ANNOUNCEMENT OF ARMAGEDDON (vv. 9-10)

Although Joel does not use the term Armageddon, he is one of the first prophets to predict its coming. "Prepare war" (v. 9) is the proclamation that will be heralded throughout the world before Armageddon. The word "prepare" means to *sanctify,* most likely referring to the Middle East custom of nations making supplication to their gods by means of a blood sacrifice before engaging in a military campaign. Many heathen nations would supplicate their gods with animal sacrifices hoping to assure victory over their enemies. At the pleading of Israel, Samuel offered supplicating sacrifice at Mizpah before they battled with the Philistines (1 Sam. 7:8-10).

The picture is one of international peace, when suddenly a declaration of war quickly permeates the world. Such terms as "... wake up the mighty men, ... men of war draw near; let them come up" (v. 9) are military terms summoning all nations to the place of battle. Even the "weak," those who would never initiate war, are stirred to present themselves as strong warriors (v. 10).

The nations are to prepare for the conflict by beating their agricultural implements into weapons, "plowshares into swords" and "pruning hooks into spears" (v. 10). During the Kingdom Age the reverse will be true (Isa. 2:4).

ASSEMBLY FOR ARMAGEDDON (vv. 11-12)

The nations are to assemble themselves (v. 11) in the Valley of Jehoshaphat (v. 12), located between Jerusalem on the east and the Mount of Olives, for the battle of Armageddon.

Although Joel mentions Jehoshaphat's valley as the place of Armageddon, three other locations are indicated too. The second place will be Mount Megiddo, "And he gathered them together into a place called in the Hebrew tongue

Armageddon" (Rev. 16:16). The word "Armageddon" is a Greek transliteration of two Hebrew words, *Har*, meaning *mountain*, and *Megiddo*, which means to *crush, kill, strike, massacre;* thus, the *mountain of desolation.* Megiddo is a mound which has been built up from the rubble of twenty cities for 3,000 years, reaching some seventy feet high. It is located at the southwest end of the Carmel mountain range, bordering the Jezreel Valley, and stretches twenty-two miles long and sixteen miles wide. Megiddo is the crossroads of the Middle East going north and south. Two major trade routes meet at the mount: the King's Highway and Via Maris (way of the sea). In 1799, Napolean Bonaparte stood on Megiddo and called it a natural battlefield.

Natural battlefield indeed! Throughout the centuries Jews, Egyptians, Persians, Crusaders, Druses, Turks and many Arabs have all fought there. It is the place where Deborah and Barak defeated the Canaanites (Jud. 4-5); Gideon defeated the Midianites (Jud. 7); Ahaziah slew Jehu (2 Ki. 9:27); and Josiah was killed by Pharaoh-neco of Egypt (2 Ki. 23:29-30). And once again the nations of the world will gather at Megiddo for the battle of Armageddon. The third area in which the battle is spoken of as taking place is Edom (Isa. 34:6; 63:1-6), located southeast of Jerusalem. The fourth location is the whole country of Judah (Zech. 12:2-11; 14:2).

Although God said He will gather all nations to battle in Israel (Joel 3:2; Zech. 14:2; Rev. 16:16), two other forces will bring the nations as well. The nations will come of their own will to overthrow the Antichrist (Dan. 11:40-44) who will have set himself in Israel as a world ruler (Rev. 13:7, 17), demanding all nations to worship him as God (Rev. 13:8, 12, 15).

Amazingly, Satan will also gather the nations to Israel. Demonic spirits will come from Satan, the Antichrist, and the false prophet, drawing the kings of the world to war through the working of miracles (Rev. 16:13-14). But why would Satan, who will be in control of Israel via the Antichrist, wish to bring the nations to Israel for battle? Notice, Satan is really drawing them ". . . to the battle of that great day of God Almighty" (Rev. 16:14).

Satan will bring them to Israel for a number of reasons. First, he will have been cast out of Heaven, meaning his access to God has been cut off (Rev. 12:9; cp. Job 1:6-12). Second, he will know that time is running out for him, and he must act quickly to destroy the divine program of God (Rev. 12:12). Third, he will want to pour out his wrath upon Israel (Rev. 12:12) hoping that her destruction (Rev. 12:6, 13, 15, 17) will keep God's program from coming to fruition. Fourth, he will gather them to destroy Christ at His second advent (Ps. 2:2-4); for if he can overthrow Christ's rule on earth, he can keep it for himself (Rev. 16:14).

AWESOMENESS OF ARMAGEDDON (vv. 13-15)

With a prophetic eye Joel sees into the future as a multitude (v. 14) of soldiers stream into the Jezreel Valley surging forth toward their destruction. The word "multitude" comes from a root word in Hebrew (hama) which means *to make a loud noise,* or *be turbulent.* The multitude of troops will produce a deafening sound as they progress into the valley of decision.

Scripture details the areas from which they will come. First, the king of the south, most likely the leader of Egypt, will come into the land with a confederacy from North Africa (Dan. 11:40). Second, the king of the north, possibly a confederacy headed by the Soviet Union (Dan. 11:40), will descend on Israel. Third, the kings of the east will sweep across the dried up Euphrates River (Rev. 16:12; Dan. 11:44) with 200,000,000 men (Rev. 9:16) to join the other nations. Fourth, the armies of western Europe will already be in the land of Israel helping the Antichrist defend his holdings.

War will break out between the military factions. What many call the battle of Armageddon will not be a single battle, but actually a war, for the word "battle" (Gr., polemos) means a *war* or *campaign* (Rev. 16:14). Although the war will center around Jerusalem (Zech. 14:2), its extent will reach out in a 200-mile radius of the city (Rev. 14:20).

Before presenting the Second Coming of Christ to judge the nations, Joel describes the actual judgment poured out upon them in the "valley of decision." The name "valley of decision" (v. 14) is a descriptive phrase indeed. The Hebrew word for "decision" (charute) has a basic meaning of *to decide,* and *sharpen* or *to cut.* Thus, it is used metaphorically in reference to God's decision to cut these huge armies into pieces as one would mow down grain with a sharp threshing sledge.

God is long-suffering with man, "not willing that any should perish, but that all should come to repentance" (2 Pet. 3:9). Yet, men despise the goodness, forbearance and long-suffering of God, thus judgment must inevitably come (Rom. 2:2-6).

Joel pictures the nations being harvested for judgment. "Put in the sickle" (v. 13), he cries. In the fourteenth chapter of Revelation, John declares that the nations are ripe for judgment. He uses two different Greek words for ripe: one speaks of the grapes as overripe and starting to wither (Rev. 14:15), and the other refers to the grapes as full grown (Rev. 14:18), at their peak for harvesting. With the help of angels, Christ thrusts in the sharp sickle, cutting down the nations in judgment (Rev. 14:14-16, 19).

The winepress is full and the vats overflow (v. 13) with the harvest. The imagery portrays grapes being trampled underfoot until all the juice is squeezed out to make wine. But here blood, not grape juice, spurts forth from the winepress of God's wrath (Rev. 14:14-20). In the day of God's vengeance, the Lord's garments will be stained with the blood of those He has slain (Isa. 63:1-3; Rev. 19:13).

The Lord will crush the nations of the world simply by the word of His mouth, leaving them to appear as if they had been put through a winepress (Rev. 19:15). The carnage will be so great that their blood will splash to the horses' bridles (about five feet high) in a radius of 200 miles (Rev. 14:20).

When the Lord speaks in judgment, the soldiers' flesh will be consumed from their bodies while they are still standing (Zech. 14:12). The word "consume" literally means *rot* in Hebrew, and has the idea of *wasting away,* as does the flesh of a leper. At Armageddon, the victim's flesh will decay rapidly from his body and fall off the bones, leaving only a skeletal image of the person.

APPEARANCE OF THE ANOINTED (vv. 15-17)

Just prior to the judgment of the Lord, Joel once again mentions the wonders that will take place in the heavens: "The sun and the moon shall be darkened, and the stars shall withdraw their shining" (v. 15; cp. Mt. 24:29; Mk. 13:24-25; Rev. 6:12-13).

The appearance of Christ for the battle of Armageddon will have three effects on men. First, they will not be able to see, because darkness will envelope them when the lights of the universe go out. Those who would not receive the light of God's Word, which provides salvation in Jesus Christ, will be left to grope in their darkness only to be destroyed "with the brightness of his coming" (2 Th. 2:8).

Second, the ear of man will be affected when "The Lord also shall roar out of Zion, and utter his voice from Jerusalem" (v. 16). While men stagger about in a desperate search for light to relieve their blind condition, the voice of the Lord rolling through the heavens, as a lion makes his presence known before devouring its prey, will strike terror in them. Those who would not open their ears to the truth of the 144,000 Jewish witnesses during the Tribulation (Rev. 7; Mt. 24:14) will be given strong delusion that they should hear and believe Satan's lie (2 Th. 2:11). With the word of His mouth and the breath of His lips, Christ will slay the nations gathered for battle (Isa. 11:4; Rev. 19:15).

Third, when Christ returns, His roar will shake "the heavens and the earth" (v. 16) in judgment. Men will feel as if the foundation and framework of creation are being destroyed. The convulsing of nature will be a sign that God's day of grace and compassion upon an ungodly world has come to an end; it will be THE DAY OF THE LORD'S JUDGMENT.

The appearance of the Lord will be awesome. Suddenly He will appear in the clouds, and the brightness of His glory will illumine the universe (Mt. 24:30). Christ will be seated on a white stallion, and on His head will be many crowns (diadems), a symbol that He is the conquering King of kings (Rev. 19:11-12, 16). His eyes will be a flame of fire, and His vesture will have been dipped in blood (Rev. 19:12-13), a picture of His penetrating judgment upon the nations. With Him will be the armies of righteousness; saints from throughout the ages and the angelic host of Heaven (Rev. 19:14).

How will the nations react at the Lord's appearing? Will they bow in humble repentance at His presence? No! "The kings of the earth set themselves, and the rulers take counsel together, against the Lord, and against his anointed [Christ]" in the hope of destroying Him (Ps. 2:2-3). But when they see Him, the tribes of the earth will mourn at the awful fate which they know awaits them (Mt. 24:30).

But what of the righteous in Israel who survive the Tribulation? ". . . the Lord will be the hope of his people, and the strength of the children of Israel" (v.16), said Joel. God will supernaturally protect a remnant of Jews from both the Antichrist and the judgment of Christ at His coming (Rev. 12:14, 17; Zech. 13:9).

When Christ destroys Israel's enemies, her eyes will be opened, and she will know that He has been her Messiah and protector all along (v. 17). By Christ's dwelling in the midst of Jerusalem, Israel will feel secure knowing that His presence assures her safety from any foreign aggressors in the future (v. 17; 2:27).

Jerusalem has been "trodden down by the Gentiles" (Lk. 21:24) for centuries, but no more will strangers oppress her, for no unrighteous person will be allowed to defile Jerusalem with his presence during the Millennial Kingdom (Rev. 21:3, 27).

Now, back to the original question purposed in this

chapter, *Will the battle of Armageddon be a nuclear holocaust which will annihilate life on this planet?* Although men will survive Armageddon, one cannot rule out nuclear warfare.

Nuclear weapons are being developed to such a degree that the possibility of their limited use to destroy a country or an army is feasible. Remember, Armageddon will not be a single battle but a campaign of battles in which vast numbers of soldiers will be destroyed before the Lord returns to earth.

World conditions give strong indication that God's prophetic clock is nearing the midnight hour when Armageddon will take place. We who know the terror of the Lord must persuade those living in constant fear of a nuclear holocaust or Armageddon that their survival is assured by putting their hope in Jesus Christ. There will be a day after! It will be a beautiful day after for all who put their faith in Jesus Christ! *Have you?*

JOEL 3:18-21

And it shall come to pass, in that day, that the mountains shall drop down new wine, and the hills shall flow with milk, and all the rivers of Judah shall flow with waters, and a fountain shall come forth from the house of the Lord, and shall water the Valley of Shittim. Egypt shall be a desolation, and Edom shall be a desolate wilderness, for the violence against the children of Judah, because they have shed innocent blood in their land. But Judah shall dwell forever, and Jerusalem from generation to generation. For I will avenge their blood that I have not avenged; for the Lord dwelleth in Zion.

FOUR HUNDRED SILENT YEARS

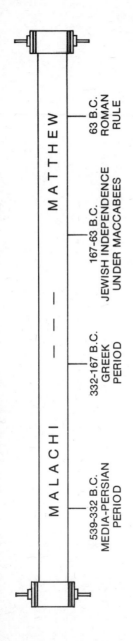

MALACHI — — — MATTHEW

539-332 B.C.
MEDIA-PERSIAN
PERIOD

332-167 B.C.
GREEK
PERIOD

167-63 B.C.
JEWISH INDEPENDENCE
UNDER MACCABEES

63 B.C.
ROMAN
RULE

THE JEWISH PEOPLE AT MESSIAH'S COMING

POLITICALLY

- Ruled by Rome

- Looking for Messiah

- Sanhedrin
  (Local government in
  Israel) has
  limited power
  under Rome

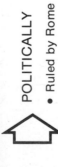

RELIGIOUSLY

- Emphasis on religious externals

- Religious Groups:
  Pharisees - legalists, self-righteous
  Sadducees - free-thinkers, worldly
  Essenes - mystic pietists, ascetics
  Believing Remnant - looked for Messiah

- Talmud developed

8

THE DAY OF THE LORD: RESTORATION IN THE MILLENNIUM

Joel 3:18-21

Towering some fifty-eight feet high is the beige limestone Wailing Wall. Standing at the wall is the stooped, five foot figure of an Orthodox Jew. Daily he comes to pray, head covered, shoulders draped in a tallith, and prayer book in hand. In Hebrew he offers a mumbled prayer for Messiah to come, bring peace to Israel, and rebuild the Temple on its historical site. Hundreds of his fellow countrymen come with the same request, written on small pieces of wadded paper, which they will stick into the crevices of the massive stone wall, hoping that the Lord will take action on their prayers.

The Jew, who has known nothing but war or the threat of it for three thousand years, longs for peace. Yet, deep in his heart, he senses that lasting peace will not come to Israel until Messiah, "The Prince of Peace" (Isa. 9:6), brings it.

With broad strokes, Joel pens an outline of the peace and blessing which Israel is to experience when Messiah sets up the Millennial Kingdom.

RESTORATION OF THE LAND (v. 18)

God gave the land of Canaan to Israel as an everlasting possession in an unconditional, eternal covenant, known as the Abrahamic Covenant (Gen. 17:7, 13, 19). The land promised to Israel during the Millennium will stretch from the river of Egypt to the Euphrates River (Gen. 15:18). When the Messiah returns He will redivide the land among the redeemed of Israel (Ezek. 48:1-7, 23-27), with a thirty-four square mile middle section set aside for the priests, Levites, Temple and Prince (Ezek. 48:8-22).

Many topographical changes will take place in the land during this time. When the Lord sets His feet on the Mount of Olives, it will cleave apart forming a huge valley east of Jerusalem (Zech. 14:4-5). The land will be transformed like the "Arabah" (Zech. 14:10), which is a geographical name for the rift that reaches from the Sea of Galilee through the Jordan Valley to the Dead Sea, an area ranging from 650-1,300 feet below sea level. Zechariah uses the comparison to show how the land will be depressed into a great plain, stretching "from Geba to Rimmon south of Jerusalem" (Zech. 14:10), the area originally given to Judah, Simeon and Benjamin. Jerusalem will be elevated and enlarged to give it an exalted position, since it is to become the geographical center of God's program. There Messiah will place the Millennial Temple and His throne (Jer. 3:17; Ezek. 43:7).

The "house of the Lord" (v. 18) has a perennial river flowing from it which will water the "Valley of Shittim" (v. 18), before emptying into the Mediterranean and Dead Seas (Zech. 14:8). The "Valley of Shittim" is a barren area of Jordan just above the Dead Sea. It is the last place Israel camped, east of Jordan, before entering into the land of Canaan (Num. 25:1; Josh. 3:1). The river will water the Judean wilderness (Isa. 35:6), with the help of heavy rainfall (Isa. 30:23; Ezek. 34:26), causing the desolate land and the solitary place to "blossom like the rose" (Isa. 35:1). The desert shall bloom forth in dense foliage like Lebanon, Mount Carmel and the coastal plains of Sharon (Isa. 35:2).

Joel described the land in figurative language as flowing with "new wine" and "milk" (v. 18), symbolic of tremendous growth and productivity during the Millennium. The climatic conditions will produce an abundance of food, so that the plowman will overtake the reaper (Dt. 30:9; Isa. 30:23-24; Amos 9:13).

The animal kingdom shall be at peace (Isa. 11:6-9) and every creature changed when the curse is lifted from the earth, except for the serpent who beguiled Eve in the garden (Gen. 3:14; Isa. 65:25).

REIGN OF THE LORD (v. 21)

The Lord will dwell in Zion upon His return to the earth (v. 21; cp. Ps. 2:6) and rule, seated upon David's throne (2 Sam. 7:16; Isa. 9:7; Lk. 1:32-33). His reign will be characterized in a number of ways. First, it will be *global,* for the Father will give Him the nations for His inheritance and the "uttermost parts of the earth for [His] possession" (Ps. 2:8). Second, His rule will be *absolute in authority and power,* for He shall rule over the nations "with a rod of iron" (Rev. 12:5; 19:15); yet He shall show mercy (Isa. 54:7-10). Third, He will be a *righteous and just ruler* (Isa. 11:3-4), for He will rule with truth (Isa. 25:1) and holiness (Ezek. 36:20-23). Fourth, *universal peace* will redound throughout the earth (Isa. 2:3-4), especially in Jerusalem (Isa. 65:18-19); for God will pour out His peace in a double portion of joy (Isa. 63:7), giving "the oil of joy for mourning" and "the garment of praise for the spirit of heaviness" (Isa. 61:3).

RESIDENTS OF THE LAND (v. 20)

When the Lord returns He will pour out His Spirit upon the house of David and Jerusalem, at which time all Israel will be saved (Zech. 12:10; Rom. 11:26). The curse of rejection, which has been on the lips of Israel through the centuries will be replaced with the cry of reception as they repent of their sins and are declared righteous in Christ (Ezek. 36:25-26; 37:23).

The Lord will bring about a spiritual reunion of the twelve tribes from among the nations of the world and forge them into one people in the land (Ezek. 37:15-22) for the first time in three thousand years.

There are four groups of people who will enter into the Millennium, three in their glorified bodies, and one in their natural bodies. Those who enter in their glorified bodies will be the Old Testament believers, the Church and the Tribulation believers who will have been martyred for their faith. The righteous who survive the Tribulation will enter in with their natural bodies to procreate and repopulate the earth, especially the Jewish people (Jer. 30:19-20).

Only the righteous will enter into the Kingdom at its inception, for the Lord will judge the nations putting the righteous (sheep) on His right hand and giving them the Kingdom prepared before the foundation of the world (Mt. 25:33-34). The unrighteous (goats) will be put on His left hand, done away with, and their destiny will be sealed to the "everlasting fire, prepared for the devil and his angels" (Mt. 25:33, 41).

Those entering the Kingdom in their natural bodies who are blind, deaf, lame and dumb will be immediately healed (Isa. 35:5-6). Most will be blessed with longevity of life since they will be free from illness (Isa. 33:24). If one dies at a hundred years of age, it will be as if he had died in childhood (Isa. 65:20).

The offspring of the righteous will have to accept the Lord, as their parents did before them; many will, but some will not. Near the end of the Kingdom, Satan, who will have been bound in the bottomless pit, will be loosed for a little season and will try to overthrow the Lord's rule through the unsaved, but God will destroy them with fire out of Heaven (Rev. 20:8-9).

A new social order will emerge in Israel and throughout the world. Jew and Gentile will be able to build houses, plant fields and reap the increase of their labor without fear of an aggressor taking it from them (Isa. 65:21-22).

RELIGION IN THE LAND

A fourth Temple will be erected in the Kingdom which is commonly called the Millennial Temple (Ezek. 40-42). The

Shekinah glory, which departed in the day of Ezekiel (Ezek. 10:3-5, 18-19; 11:23), will again descend upon this Temple through the East Gate (Ezek. 43:1-5) making it holy.

During the Millennium, worship will be reestablished on the Sabbath and animal sacrifice will be offered once again in the new Temple (Ezek. 46). Two questions arise concerning animal sacrifices to be offered at this time. First, *If the priesthood was destroyed in A.D. 70, from where do the priests come who will lead in worship and offer sacrifices?* Israel will take men from the tribe of Levi by the name of Cohen and Levy to be used in the Temple worship (Ezek. 44:9-31). The name Cohen (Heb., Kohen) means *priest,* and the name Levy (Heb., Levi) were those who served in the Temple along with the priests.

Many ask, *Why will animal sacrifices be offered since the Lord has once and for all entered into the holy place having obtained eternal redemption (Heb. 9:12) through His blood for mankind?* The sacrifices cannot be efficacious, for the blood of bulls and goats could never take away sin but were only a covering for it (Heb. 10:4). It is reasonable to assume that these sacrifices will be a memorial offering, similar to the Lord's table, done in remembrance of Christ's atoning sacrifice on the cross.

During this time Jews will be called "the Ministers of our God" (Isa. 61:6) and will function as spiritual leaders under the Lord's direction. It will be their ministry to proclaim Messiah's glory among the nations (Isa. 66:19-20). In that day, ten men out of every nation will grab hold of a Jew desiring to be taught about the Lord from him (Zech. 8:23).

The nations of the world will be expected to make a yearly pilgrimage to Jerusalem for the purpose of worshipping the Lord and keeping the Feast of Tabernacles (Zech. 14:16). Those refusing to come will have rain withheld from them (Zech. 14:17). If the Egyptians come not up, they will suffer plagues (Zech. 14:18), since they depend on the annual overflow of the Nile River to water their crops, rather than rain.

Like Israel, the Church will be made a kingdom of priests (Rev. 1:6) and will be given authority to reign with the Lord, most likely serving Him among the nations (Rev. 2:26-27). Scripture seems to indicate that Christians who are given leadership in the Kingdom will rule and reign over Gentile cities (Lk. 19:17-19), while the apostles are to be seated on thrones to judge the twelve tribes of Israel (Mt. 19:28; Lk. 22:28-30).

In the Kingdom, God will answer the prayers of Jewish people and others, before they ask in some cases, and in other instances while the request is being made (Isa. 65:24).

REVENGE ON OTHER LANDS (vv. 19, 21)

God has promised to avenge Judah for the injustice suffered at the hands of the Egyptians and the Edomites (vv. 19, 21).

EGYPT

From the inception of Jacob's descent into Goshen (Gen. 46:1-27) until the present day, Egypt has cast a long shadow over Israel's history through entangled treaties and military ventures. Whenever Israel leaned on Egypt for help, she proved to be a cracked staff, providing little or no support (Ezek. 29:7).

The prophets of Judah continually predicted the fall of Egypt, because of the way she treated Israel (Isa. 19; Ezek. 29). Although she has risen from the dust of destruction, Egypt will remain a second-rate nation (Ezek. 29:14) until the Millennium.

Like an echo, history will be repeated, for Egypt will be downtrodden and subdued by the Antichrist during the Great Tribulation (Dan. 11:43). Egypt's future looks bleak, but not all is doom and gloom, for she will experience restoration and great blessing in the Millennium. Five major Egyptian cities will speak the language of Canaan and be committed to the Lord of hosts (Isa. 19:18), which indicates that they will be converted.

An altar and pillar will be erected in Egypt (Isa. 19:19). The altar is for memorial sacrifices like the ones offered in the Millennial Temple; and the pillar will be a sign and witness that Egypt has put faith in the Lord.

A highway will extend from Assyria to Egypt, running through Israel. The highway will symbolize the new relationship that exists between these three nations. Egypt and Assyria, so often at war down through the centuries, will be forged into a spiritual alliance along with Israel (Isa. 19:23). Egypt will be called "my people," a title limited to Israel until now, and Assyria is referred to as the "work" of God's hands, while Israel is declared the "inheritance" of the Lord (Isa. 19:25). Even though desolation is predicted on Egypt, her resurrection and spiritual renewal are forthcoming.

EDOM

Edom was the name given to the land southeast of Judah where Esau and his descendents settled. It extends from the Dead Sea to the Gulf of Aqaba, bordered on the west by the valley of Arabah, on the east by a large mountain range, and on the north by Moab. Edom is best known for the rose-colored city of Petra which was hewn from solid rock, tucked away for centuries in the center of the land. The city was situated in a direct line between Egypt and Babylon which became a major trade route called the King's Highway. Petra was a natural stopping place for caravans traveling on the highway. Although Edom is a desolate, rugged and almost inaccessible area, at one time it was a very cultivated area enjoying the "fatness of the earth, and of the dew of heaven" (Gen. 27:39; cp. Num. 20:17).

Esau's bitter hatred for his brother Jacob was passed down through the centuries to the Edomites (Ex. 15:15; Num. 20:14ff; Ps. 83:6) who persecuted Israel.

Edom and Israel have been vicious enemies throughout the centuries. The conflict began when Edom would not allow Israel access to travel up the highway from Sinai to Kadesh-barnea (Num. 20:14-22). Later, Edom was defeated by Saul, David and Joab who almost destroyed all the male population (1 Ki. 11:15-16). Jehoshaphat defeated them in the valley of Beracah (2 Chr. 20:22). Although Amaziah captured Petra (2 Ki. 14:7; 2 Chr. 25:11-12), Israel was never able to completely subdue Edom (2 Chr. 28:17).

When the Babylonians destroyed Jerusalem, the Edomites took an aggressive part in plundering the city and killing the Jewish population (Ps. 137:7; Obad. 10-14). Because of Edom's treatment toward Judah, the prophets pronounced horrible judgments which would befall her (Isa. 34:5-8; 63:1-4; Jer. 49:17; Lam. 4:21; Ezek. 25:13-14).

Today Edom is a desolate wilderness as Joel predicted. Once again Edom will face the hand of God's wrath during *the day of the Lord* for their treatment of Israel (Obad. 15-21) and remain a "desolate wilderness" (v. 19) during the Millennium.

Joel has graphically portrayed that Israel has and will pay double (Jer. 16:18) for her sins during *the day of the Lord.* She will also become an *astonishment,* dumbfounding the nations who will stand in bewilderment at the unprecedented fall and calamities that will come upon her after reaching such heights before God. Israel did become a *byword,* suffering from the most cutting sarcasm that could befall any nation down through the centuries, as nation after nation spewed out blasphemous verbage about her. God allowed the Jew to become a *proverb* among the nations, using her as a public example and object lesson of how He will discipline those who continue to be disobedient toward His loving grace.

Yet, *the day of the Lord* is to be a time of blessing for Israel when God will answer the fervent prayers of so many who have wept at the Wailing Wall. The day will come when God says, *Enough!* Once again He will speak tenderly to Jerusalem revealing that her warfare is accomplished, and her iniquity has been pardoned (Isa. 40:2). This will become a reality when the Lord comes the second time to set up the Kingdom.

EPILOGUE:
WHAT NEXT?

Joel has answered many questions concerning Israel's prophetic history, but one still remains in the reader's mind: Exactly when will *the day of the Lord* begin in order for end time prophecies to be fulfilled? No exact date is possible, since *the day of the Lord* begins after the Church is raptured. But biblical prophecy casts shadows. Thus, one can get some indication of God's prophetic time line by comparing prophecy with world events.

The world stage is being set, and the curtain is about to rise on the final act of God's program. A number of prophetic props are being set on the world stage. First, Israel is back in her land as a self-governing people for the first time in nineteen centuries. Israel must be in her land during *the day of the Lord.* Second, ten common market nations have confederated together in Europe, which could be a precursor to the revival of the Roman Empire, a ten-nation confederacy prophesied in Daniel and Revelation. Third, Russia has become a superpower north of the Middle East and is poised to strike against Israel as prophesied in Ezekiel 38-39. Fourth, as world tensions grow to a fever pitch, nations are looking for a man who will provide direction to stave off a seething pot of global conflict which could erupt into World War III. During *the day of the Lord* a man called the Antichrist will emerge as a world ruler. His ultimate goal will be to dominate the world and be worshiped as God (Rev. 13; 2 Th. 2:4), but his desire will never come to fruition. Fifth, the perilous times mentioned in 2 Timothy 3:1-5 are being manifested worldwide as never before.

Even the nonreligious man senses that something major is about to happen worldwide. Many are fearing a nuclear holocaust that would bring massive destruction and possibly annihilate life on this planet. Something big is in the wind, but it is not nuclear annihilation. It is a time of unprecedented tribulation which will sweep the earth after the Church is raptured.

With big brush strokes, God has painted a time line of prophetic events which give indication that the Tribulation is near. How near? One cannot be certain, but world conditions indicate that this age is swiftly coming to a culmination and *the day of the Lord* cannot be far off. For example, when spring buds out in all of its beauty, one knows that summer is right behind; or after enjoying the bounty of Thanksgiving day, all know that Christmas will soon be celebrated.

Since *the day of the Lord* could be imminent, what is man to do? Man's hope is found in Jesus Christ who provides the only means to escape the terrible Tribulation that is to sweep the earth. If you have not done so, right now, simply repent of your sins and receive Christ as your Savior and Lord. Having made this commitment, you can be assured that your sins are forgiven and Christ has given you eternal life (1 Jn. 5:11-13).

Since *the day of the Lord* could be imminent, what is the believer to do? First, watch and wait, making sure he is spiritually ready for the imminent return of Christ.

Second, he is to "occupy" (Lk. 19:13) until Christ comes. The Lord used the word "occupy" in the parable of the ten pounds (Lk. 19:11-27) to show His followers that they were expected to work until His return.

The story goes like this. A nobleman, before going on a long journey, gave ten servants ten pounds each and asked them to gain more for him by *occupying,* or trading in the market place. When the nobleman returned, he would call his servants to give an account of their stewardship. The spiritual application is clear. The believer is to "occupy," or do spiritual business in the market place, by using his God-given gifts to produce fruit until Christ comes for His Church.

Knowing the Lord will hold him accountable for his stewardship, the believer should be busy redeeming the time, buying up every spiritual opportunity to proclaim and teach the gospel to a lost and dying world.

The day of the Lord is imminent. Will you accept the challenge in these last days to give all-out service to the Lord? Remember, "it is required in stewards, that a man be found faithful" (1 Cor. 4:2).

FOOTNOTES

Chapter 1

1. Merrill F. Unger, *Unger's Bible Dictionary*, (Chicago: Moody Press, 1957), pp. 61-62.

2. Spiros Zodhiates, *Pulpit Helps*, (Chattanooga: AMG Publishers).

Chapter 2

1. J.J. Given, *The Pulpit Commentary, Daniel, Hosea, and Joel*, (Grand Rapids: Wm. B. Eerdman Publishing Co., 1950), Vol. XIII, p. 20.

2. E.B. Pusey, *The Minor Prophets: A Commentary*, (Grand Rapids: Baker Book House, 1950), Vol. I, p. 174.

3. Ibid., p. 175.

4. Ibid., p. 177.

Chapter 4

1. Pusey, op. cit., p. 189.

2. Hobart E. Freeman, *An Introduction to the Old Testament Prophets*, (Chicago: Moody Press, 1968), p. 153.

3. *Congressional Quarterly*, The Middle East U.S. Policy, Israel, Oil, and the Arabs, Third Edition, Chronology 1975, (Washington: Congressional Quarterly Inc., 1977), p. 177.

4. *Myths and Facts 1976, A Concise Record of the Arab-*

Israeli Conflict, (Washington: Near East Report, 1976), p. 64.

Chapter 5

1. Freeman, op. cit., p. 150-53. Concept of the various positions are mentioned in this book.

Chapter 6

1. Pusey, op. cit., p. 206.

2. Charles L. Feinberg, *The Major Messages of the Minor Prophets: Joel, Amos, and Obadiah,* (New York: American Board of Missions to the Jews, Inc., 1948), p. 33.

BIBLIOGRAPHY

Congressional Quarterly, The Middle East U.S. Policy, Israel, Oil, and the Arabs. Third Edition. Chronology 1975. Washington: Congressional Quarterly Inc., 1977.

Feinberg, Charles L. *The Major Messages of the Minor Prophets: Joel, Amos, and Obadiah.* New York: American Board of Missions to the Jews, Inc. 1948.

Freeman, Hobart E. *An Introduction to the Old Testament Prophets.* Chicago: Moody Press, 1968.

Given, J.J. *The Pulpit Commentary, Daniel, Hosea, and Joel.* Vol. III. Grand Rapids: Wm. B. Eerdman Publishing Co., 1950.

Myths and Facts 1976. A Concise Record of the Arab-Israeli Conflict, Washington: Near East Report, 1976.

Pusey, E.B. *The Minor Prophets: A Commentary.* Vol. I. Grand Rapids: Baker Book House, 1950.

Unger, Merrill F. *Bible Dictionary.* Chicago: Moody Press, 1957.

Zodhiates, Spiros. *Pulpit Helps.* Chattanooga: AMG Publishers.